Blockchain Solutions
Complete Self-Assessment Guide

C000015865

The guidance in this Self-Assessment is based o͏ͅ ͏ͅ͏ͅ͏ͅ
best practices and standards in business process architecture, design
and quality management. The guidance is also based on the professional
judgment of the individual collaborators listed in the Acknowledgments.

Notice of rights

Table of Contents

About The Art of Service

The Art of Service, Business Process Architects since 2000, is dedicated to helping stakeholders achieve excellence.

Defining, designing, creating, and implementing a process to solve a stakeholders challenge or meet an objective is the most valuable role… In EVERY group, company, organization and department.

Unless you're talking a one-time, single-use project, there should be a process. Whether that process is managed and implemented by humans, AI, or a combination of the two, it needs to be designed by someone with a complex enough perspective to ask the right questions.

Someone capable of asking the right questions and step back and say, 'What are we really trying to accomplish here? And is there a different way to look at it?'

With The Art of Service's Standard Requirements Self-Assessments, we empower people who can do just that — whether their title is marketer, entrepreneur, manager, salesperson, consultant, Business Process Manager, executive assistant, IT Manager, CIO etc... —they are the people who rule the future. They are people who watch the process as it happens, and ask the right questions to make the process work better.

Contact us when you need any support with this Self-Assessment and any help with templates, blue-prints and examples of standard documents you might need:

http://theartofservice.com
service@theartofservice.com

Included Resources - how to access

Included with your purchase of the book is the Blockchain

Solutions Self-Assessment Spreadsheet Dashboard which contains all questions and Self-Assessment areas and auto-generates insights, graphs, and project RACI planning - all with examples to get you started right away.

How? Simply send an email to
access@theartofservice.com
with this books' title in the subject to get the Blockchain Solutions Self Assessment Tool right away.

You will receive the following contents with New and Updated specific criteria:

- The latest quick edition of the book in PDF

- The latest complete edition of the book in PDF, which criteria correspond to the criteria in...

- The Self-Assessment Excel Dashboard, and...

- Example pre-filled Self-Assessment Excel Dashboard to get familiar with results generation

- In-depth specific Checklists covering the topic

- Project management checklists and templates to assist with implementation

INCLUDES LIFETIME SELF ASSESSMENT UPDATES

Every self assessment comes with Lifetime Updates and Lifetime Free Updated Books. Lifetime Updates is an industry-first feature which allows you to receive verified self assessment updates, ensuring you always have the most accurate information at your fingertips.

Get it now- you will be glad you did - do it now, before you forget.

Send an email to **access@theartofservice.com** with this books' title in the subject to get the Blockchain Solutions Self Assessment Tool right away.

Purpose of this Self-Assessment

This Self-Assessment has been developed to improve understanding of the requirements and elements of Blockchain Solutions, based on best practices and standards in business process architecture, design and quality management.

It is designed to allow for a rapid Self-Assessment to determine how closely existing management practices and procedures correspond to the elements of the Self-Assessment.

The criteria of requirements and elements of Blockchain Solutions have been rephrased in the format of a Self-Assessment questionnaire, with a seven-criterion scoring system, as explained in this document.

In this format, even with limited background knowledge of Blockchain Solutions, a manager can quickly review existing operations to determine how they measure up to the standards. This in turn can serve as the starting point of a 'gap analysis' to identify management tools or system elements that might usefully be implemented in the organization to help improve overall performance.

How to use the Self-Assessment

On the following pages are a series of questions to identify to what extent your Blockchain Solutions initiative is complete in comparison to the requirements set in standards.

To facilitate answering the questions, there is a space in front of each question to enter a score on a scale of '1' to '5'.

1 Strongly Disagree

2 Disagree

3 Neutral

4 Agree

5 Strongly Agree

Read the question and rate it with the following in front of mind:

'In my belief, the answer to this question is clearly defined'.

There are two ways in which you can choose to interpret this statement;
1. how aware are you that the answer to the question is clearly defined
2. for more in-depth analysis you can choose to gather evidence and confirm the answer to the question. This obviously will take more time, most Self-Assessment users opt for the first way to interpret the question and dig deeper later on based on the outcome of the overall Self-Assessment.

A score of '1' would mean that the answer is not clear at all, where a '5' would mean the answer is crystal clear and defined. Leave emtpy when the question is not applicable or you don't want to answer it, you can skip it without affecting your score. Write your score in the space provided.

After you have responded to all the appropriate statements in each section, compute your average score for that section, using the formula provided, and round to the nearest tenth. Then transfer to the corresponding spoke in the Blockchain Solutions Scorecard on the second next page of the Self-Assessment.

Your completed Blockchain Solutions Scorecard will give you a clear presentation of which Blockchain Solutions areas need attention.

Blockchain Solutions Scorecard Example

Example of how the finalized Scorecard can look like:

Blockchain Solutions Scorecard

Your Scores:

BEGINNING OF THE SELF-ASSESSMENT:

CRITERION #1: RECOGNIZE

1. What does Blockchain Solutions success mean to the stakeholders?
<--- Score

2. Will new equipment/products be required to facilitate Blockchain Solutions delivery, for example is new software needed?
<--- Score

3. What activities does the governance board need to consider?
<--- Score

4. How many trainings, in total, are needed?
<--- Score

5. Are controls defined to recognize and contain problems?
<--- Score

6. Who needs to know about Blockchain Solutions?
<--- Score

7. How do you recognize an objection?
<--- Score

8. Does the problem have ethical dimensions?
<--- Score

9. Have you identified your Blockchain Solutions key performance indicators?
<--- Score

10. Think about the people you identified for your Blockchain Solutions project and the project responsibilities you would assign to them, what kind of training do you think they would need to perform these responsibilities effectively?
<--- Score

11. What Blockchain Solutions coordination do you need?
<--- Score

12. What is the recognized need?

<--- Score

13. How can auditing be a preventative security measure?
<--- Score

14. What are the expected benefits of Blockchain Solutions to the stakeholder?
<--- Score

15. Do you need different information or graphics?
<--- Score

16. Do you need to avoid or amend any Blockchain Solutions activities?
<--- Score

17. As a sponsor, customer or management, how important is it to meet goals, objectives?
<--- Score

18. Who needs what information?
<--- Score

19. Do you know what you need to know about Blockchain Solutions?
<--- Score

20. How do you assess your Blockchain Solutions workforce capability and capacity needs, including skills, competencies, and staffing levels?
<--- Score

21. Where is training needed?
<--- Score

22. Where do you need to exercise leadership?
<--- Score

23. Does Blockchain Solutions create potential expectations in other areas that need to be recognized and considered?
<--- Score

24. What Blockchain Solutions capabilities do you need?
<--- Score

25. Are there regulatory / compliance issues?
<--- Score

26. Will it solve real problems?
<--- Score

27. For your Blockchain Solutions project, identify and describe the business environment, is there more than one layer to the business environment?
<--- Score

28. Consider your own Blockchain Solutions project, what types of organizational problems do you think might be causing or affecting your problem, based on the work done so far?
<--- Score

29. How do you identify subcontractor relationships?
<--- Score

30. What is the Blockchain Solutions problem definition? What do you need to resolve?
<--- Score

31. What are the Blockchain Solutions resources needed?
<--- Score

32. Who else hopes to benefit from it?
<--- Score

33. Are losses recognized in a timely manner?
<--- Score

34. What information do users need?
<--- Score

35. Why the need?
<--- Score

36. What needs to stay?
<--- Score

37. What are your needs in relation to Blockchain Solutions skills, labor, equipment, and markets?
<--- Score

38. Are you dealing with any of the same issues today as yesterday? What can you do about this?
<--- Score

39. Will Blockchain Solutions deliverables need to be tested and, if so, by whom?
<--- Score

40. Are there Blockchain Solutions problems defined?
<--- Score

41. What are the stakeholder objectives to be achieved with Blockchain Solutions?

<--- Score

42. What should be considered when identifying available resources, constraints, and deadlines?
<--- Score

43. What Blockchain Solutions problem should be solved?
<--- Score

44. Which issues are too important to ignore?
<--- Score

45. How much are sponsors, customers, partners, stakeholders involved in Blockchain Solutions? In other words, what are the risks, if Blockchain Solutions does not deliver successfully?
<--- Score

46. What are the minority interests and what amount of minority interests can be recognized?
<--- Score

47. What are the clients issues and concerns?
<--- Score

48. Is it needed?
<--- Score

49. Who are your key stakeholders who need to sign off?
<--- Score

50. Would you recognize a threat from the inside?
<--- Score

51. What resources or support might you need?
<--- Score

52. What would happen if Blockchain Solutions weren't done?
<--- Score

53. How are you going to measure success?
<--- Score

54. Are your goals realistic? Do you need to redefine your problem? Perhaps the problem has changed or maybe you have reached your goal and need to set a new one?
<--- Score

55. Will a response program recognize when a crisis occurs and provide some level of response?
<--- Score

56. Are there recognized Blockchain Solutions problems?
<--- Score

57. Which needs are not included or involved?
<--- Score

58. How do you recognize an Blockchain Solutions objection?
<--- Score

59. How do you identify the kinds of information that you will need?
<--- Score

60. Are there any specific expectations or concerns

about the Blockchain Solutions team, Blockchain Solutions itself?

<--- Score

61. What is the extent or complexity of the Blockchain Solutions problem?

<--- Score

62. To what extent does each concerned units management team recognize Blockchain Solutions as an effective investment?

<--- Score

63. Who defines the rules in relation to any given issue?

<--- Score

64. Is the quality assurance team identified?

<--- Score

65. How are training requirements identified?

<--- Score

66. Can management personnel recognize the monetary benefit of Blockchain Solutions?

<--- Score

67. What vendors make products that address the Blockchain Solutions needs?

<--- Score

68. To what extent would your organization benefit from being recognized as a award recipient?

<--- Score

69. What else needs to be measured?

<--- Score

70. Who should resolve the Blockchain Solutions issues?
<--- Score

71. How are the Blockchain Solutions's objectives aligned to the group's overall stakeholder strategy?
<--- Score

72. What do employees need in the short term?
<--- Score

73. Are employees recognized for desired behaviors?
<--- Score

74. What problems are you facing and how do you consider Blockchain Solutions will circumvent those obstacles?
<--- Score

75. What extra resources will you need?
<--- Score

76. Whom do you really need or want to serve?
<--- Score

77. What are the timeframes required to resolve each of the issues/problems?
<--- Score

78. Which information does the Blockchain Solutions business case need to include?
<--- Score

79. What do you need to start doing?

<--- Score

80. Does your organization need more Blockchain Solutions education?
<--- Score

81. What is the smallest subset of the problem you can usefully solve?
<--- Score

82. Looking at each person individually – does every one have the qualities which are needed to work in this group?
<--- Score

83. What is the problem and/or vulnerability?
<--- Score

84. Is the need for organizational change recognized?
<--- Score

85. What training and capacity building actions are needed to implement proposed reforms?
<--- Score

86. Why is this needed?
<--- Score

87. How does it fit into your organizational needs and tasks?
<--- Score

88. Do you recognize Blockchain Solutions achievements?
<--- Score

89. What prevents you from making the changes you know will make you a more effective Blockchain Solutions leader?
<--- Score

90. Are problem definition and motivation clearly presented?
<--- Score

91. What needs to be done?
<--- Score

92. What situation(s) led to this Blockchain Solutions Self Assessment?
<--- Score

93. Are employees recognized or rewarded for performance that demonstrates the highest levels of integrity?
<--- Score

94. What Blockchain Solutions events should you attend?
<--- Score

95. Did you miss any major Blockchain Solutions issues?
<--- Score

96. Who needs to know?
<--- Score

97. Do you have/need 24-hour access to key personnel?
<--- Score

98. When a Blockchain Solutions manager recognizes a problem, what options are available?
<--- Score

99. How do you take a forward-looking perspective in identifying Blockchain Solutions research related to market response and models?
<--- Score

100. What is the problem or issue?
<--- Score

Add up total points for this section:
_ _ _ _ _ = Total points for this section

Divided by: _ _ _ _ _ _ (number of statements answered) = _ _ _ _ _ _
Average score for this section

Transfer your score to the Blockchain Solutions Index at the beginning of the Self-Assessment.

CRITERION #2: DEFINE:

INTENT: Formulate the stakeholder problem. Define the problem, needs and objectives.

In my belief, the answer to this question is clearly defined:

5 Strongly Agree

4 Agree

3 Neutral

2 Disagree

1 Strongly Disagree

1. How do you hand over Blockchain Solutions context?
<--- Score

2. Are different versions of process maps needed to account for the different types of inputs?
<--- Score

3. What specifically is the problem? Where does it

occur? When does it occur? What is its extent?
<--- Score

4. What are the core elements of the Blockchain Solutions business case?
<--- Score

5. In what way can you redefine the criteria of choice clients have in your category in your favor?
<--- Score

6. Is the improvement team aware of the different versions of a process: what they think it is vs. what it actually is vs. what it should be vs. what it could be?
<--- Score

7. Has a project plan, Gantt chart, or similar been developed/completed?
<--- Score

8. What is the worst case scenario?
<--- Score

9. What critical content must be communicated – who, what, when, where, and how?
<--- Score

10. How do you keep key subject matter experts in the loop?
<--- Score

11. Have specific policy objectives been defined?
<--- Score

12. What information should you gather?
<--- Score

13. Is the team adequately staffed with the desired cross-functionality? If not, what additional resources are available to the team?
<--- Score

14. What sources do you use to gather information for a Blockchain Solutions study?
<--- Score

15. How is the team tracking and documenting its work?
<--- Score

16. Have all of the relationships been defined properly?
<--- Score

17. Has a team charter been developed and communicated?
<--- Score

18. Are the Blockchain Solutions requirements complete?
<--- Score

19. What Blockchain Solutions requirements should be gathered?
<--- Score

20. Are there any constraints known that bear on the ability to perform Blockchain Solutions work? How is the team addressing them?
<--- Score

21. Are resources adequate for the scope?

<--- Score

22. How was the 'as is' process map developed, reviewed, verified and validated?
<--- Score

23. Why are you doing Blockchain Solutions and what is the scope?
<--- Score

24. What Blockchain Solutions services do you require?
<--- Score

25. What key stakeholder process output measure(s) does Blockchain Solutions leverage and how?
<--- Score

26. What are the tasks and definitions?
<--- Score

27. Are approval levels defined for contracts and supplements to contracts?
<--- Score

28. Do you all define Blockchain Solutions in the same way?
<--- Score

29. How do you manage scope?
<--- Score

30. Is Blockchain Solutions currently on schedule according to the plan?
<--- Score

31. Where can you gather more information?
<--- Score

32. Has a Blockchain Solutions requirement not been met?
<--- Score

33. How and when will the baselines be defined?
<--- Score

34. Is there a Blockchain Solutions management charter, including stakeholder case, problem and goal statements, scope, milestones, roles and responsibilities, communication plan?
<--- Score

35. How would you define Blockchain Solutions leadership?
<--- Score

36. Is Blockchain Solutions required?
<--- Score

37. What are the record-keeping requirements of Blockchain Solutions activities?
<--- Score

38. When are meeting minutes sent out? Who is on the distribution list?
<--- Score

39. If substitutes have been appointed, have they been briefed on the Blockchain Solutions goals and received regular communications as to the progress to date?
<--- Score

40. What is the scope of Blockchain Solutions?
<--- Score

41. Has/have the customer(s) been identified?
<--- Score

42. Does the team have regular meetings?
<--- Score

43. What are the dynamics of the communication plan?
<--- Score

44. How do you manage unclear Blockchain Solutions requirements?
<--- Score

45. How do you catch Blockchain Solutions definition inconsistencies?
<--- Score

46. How do you manage changes in Blockchain Solutions requirements?
<--- Score

47. Are roles and responsibilities formally defined?
<--- Score

48. Has the improvement team collected the 'voice of the customer' (obtained feedback – qualitative and quantitative)?
<--- Score

49. How would you define the culture at your organization, how susceptible is it to Blockchain

Solutions changes?
<--- Score

50. Are audit criteria, scope, frequency and methods defined?
<--- Score

51. Do you have organizational privacy requirements?
<--- Score

52. The political context: who holds power?
<--- Score

53. What are the Blockchain Solutions tasks and definitions?
<--- Score

54. What constraints exist that might impact the team?
<--- Score

55. Are the Blockchain Solutions requirements testable?
<--- Score

56. Have the customer needs been translated into specific, measurable requirements? How?
<--- Score

57. Has a high-level 'as is' process map been completed, verified and validated?
<--- Score

58. How do you gather the stories?
<--- Score

59. How can the value of Blockchain Solutions be defined?
<--- Score

60. What is the scope of the Blockchain Solutions effort?
<--- Score

61. How do you think the partners involved in Blockchain Solutions would have defined success?
<--- Score

62. What are the rough order estimates on cost savings/opportunities that Blockchain Solutions brings?
<--- Score

63. What customer feedback methods were used to solicit their input?
<--- Score

64. What is the scope of the Blockchain Solutions work?
<--- Score

65. What is out of scope?
<--- Score

66. Has everyone on the team, including the team leaders, been properly trained?
<--- Score

67. What system do you use for gathering Blockchain Solutions information?
<--- Score

68. What is in scope?
<--- Score

69. Does the scope remain the same?
<--- Score

70. Are task requirements clearly defined?
<--- Score

71. What are the compelling stakeholder reasons for embarking on Blockchain Solutions?
<--- Score

72. Is scope creep really all bad news?
<--- Score

73. Do you have a Blockchain Solutions success story or case study ready to tell and share?
<--- Score

74. How will the Blockchain Solutions team and the group measure complete success of Blockchain Solutions?
<--- Score

75. How do you gather Blockchain Solutions requirements?
<--- Score

76. Is the work to date meeting requirements?
<--- Score

77. What is in the scope and what is not in scope?
<--- Score

78. Is there regularly 100% attendance at the

team meetings? If not, have appointed substitutes attended to preserve cross-functionality and full representation?

<--- Score

79. What would be the goal or target for a Blockchain Solutions's improvement team?

<--- Score

80. Has your scope been defined?

<--- Score

81. What are the Blockchain Solutions use cases?

<--- Score

82. What sort of initial information to gather?

<--- Score

83. What is the context?

<--- Score

84. Is the current 'as is' process being followed? If not, what are the discrepancies?

<--- Score

85. Is it clearly defined in and to your organization what you do?

<--- Score

86. How are consistent Blockchain Solutions definitions important?

<--- Score

87. How have you defined all Blockchain Solutions requirements first?

<--- Score

88. Who defines (or who defined) the rules and roles?
<--- Score

89. Has the Blockchain Solutions work been fairly and/or equitably divided and delegated among team members who are qualified and capable to perform the work? Has everyone contributed?
<--- Score

90. Is there a clear Blockchain Solutions case definition?
<--- Score

91. Who approved the Blockchain Solutions scope?
<--- Score

92. Will a Blockchain Solutions production readiness review be required?
<--- Score

93. Are accountability and ownership for Blockchain Solutions clearly defined?
<--- Score

94. Is there a critical path to deliver Blockchain Solutions results?
<--- Score

95. How often are the team meetings?
<--- Score

96. Has the direction changed at all during the course of Blockchain Solutions? If so, when did it change and why?
<--- Score

97. How did the Blockchain Solutions manager receive input to the development of a Blockchain Solutions improvement plan and the estimated completion dates/times of each activity?
<--- Score

98. Who is gathering information?
<--- Score

99. Is there any additional Blockchain Solutions definition of success?
<--- Score

100. Is the scope of Blockchain Solutions defined?
<--- Score

101. How do you gather requirements?
<--- Score

102. What is the definition of success?
<--- Score

103. Are there different segments of customers?
<--- Score

104. Is there a completed SIPOC representation, describing the Suppliers, Inputs, Process, Outputs, and Customers?
<--- Score

105. How do you build the right business case?
<--- Score

106. What is a worst-case scenario for losses?
<--- Score

107. What are (control) requirements for Blockchain Solutions Information?
<--- Score

108. What intelligence can you gather?
<--- Score

109. How will variation in the actual durations of each activity be dealt with to ensure that the expected Blockchain Solutions results are met?
<--- Score

110. What gets examined?
<--- Score

111. Is the Blockchain Solutions scope manageable?
<--- Score

112. Has anyone else (internal or external to the group) attempted to solve this problem or a similar one before? If so, what knowledge can be leveraged from these previous efforts?
<--- Score

113. What defines best in class?
<--- Score

114. What information do you gather?
<--- Score

115. What are the boundaries of the scope? What is in bounds and what is not? What is the start point? What is the stop point?
<--- Score

116. Is Blockchain Solutions linked to key stakeholder goals and objectives?
<--- Score

117. Who is gathering Blockchain Solutions information?
<--- Score

118. When is/was the Blockchain Solutions start date?
<--- Score

119. Have all basic functions of Blockchain Solutions been defined?
<--- Score

120. Is special Blockchain Solutions user knowledge required?
<--- Score

121. What happens if Blockchain Solutions's scope changes?
<--- Score

122. Is there a completed, verified, and validated high-level 'as is' (not 'should be' or 'could be') stakeholder process map?
<--- Score

123. Who are the Blockchain Solutions improvement team members, including Management Leads and Coaches?
<--- Score

124. Do the problem and goal statements meet the SMART criteria (specific, measurable, attainable, relevant, and time-bound)?

<--- Score

125. Is the Blockchain Solutions scope complete and appropriately sized?
<--- Score

126. What was the context?
<--- Score

127. What scope to assess?
<--- Score

128. What are the Roles and Responsibilities for each team member and its leadership? Where is this documented?
<--- Score

129. Scope of sensitive information?
<--- Score

130. What knowledge or experience is required?
<--- Score

131. How does the Blockchain Solutions manager ensure against scope creep?
<--- Score

132. Are required metrics defined, what are they?
<--- Score

133. When is the estimated completion date?
<--- Score

Add up total points for this section:
_ _ _ _ _ = Total points for this section

Divided by: _____ (number of
statements answered) = _____
Average score for this section

Transfer your score to the Blockchain
Solutions Index at the beginning of the
Self-Assessment.

CRITERION #3: MEASURE:

In my belief, the answer to this
question is clearly defined:

5 Strongly Agree

4 Agree

3 Neutral

2 Disagree

1 Strongly Disagree

1. What causes investor action?
<--- Score

2. How can you reduce the costs of obtaining inputs?
<--- Score

3. Are there competing Blockchain Solutions
priorities?
<--- Score

4. Why do the measurements/indicators matter?
<--- Score

5. What measurements are possible, practicable and meaningful?
<--- Score

6. Is the solution cost-effective?
<--- Score

7. What is your decision requirements diagram?
<--- Score

8. Are you aware of what could cause a problem?
<--- Score

9. How is progress measured?
<--- Score

10. How do you verify and develop ideas and innovations?
<--- Score

11. How are measurements made?
<--- Score

12. Have you made assumptions about the shape of the future, particularly its impact on your customers and competitors?
<--- Score

13. What happens if cost savings do not materialize?
<--- Score

14. Are actual costs in line with budgeted costs?

<--- Score

15. What is the Blockchain Solutions business impact?
<--- Score

16. Where is it measured?
<--- Score

17. Who pays the cost?
<--- Score

18. What would be a real cause for concern?
<--- Score

19. What could cause delays in the schedule?
<--- Score

20. How do you verify the authenticity of the data and information used?
<--- Score

21. Have you included everything in your Blockchain Solutions cost models?
<--- Score

22. Where is the cost?
<--- Score

23. What are the Blockchain Solutions key cost drivers?
<--- Score

24. Who should receive measurement reports?
<--- Score

25. Did you tackle the cause or the symptom?

<--- Score

26. What evidence is there and what is measured?
<--- Score

27. What are the uncertainties surrounding estimates of impact?
<--- Score

28. What methods are feasible and acceptable to estimate the impact of reforms?
<--- Score

29. What is the cause of any Blockchain Solutions gaps?
<--- Score

30. How is the value delivered by Blockchain Solutions being measured?
<--- Score

31. Are there any easy-to-implement alternatives to Blockchain Solutions? Sometimes other solutions are available that do not require the cost implications of a full-blown project?
<--- Score

32. How frequently do you track Blockchain Solutions measures?
<--- Score

33. What is the total fixed cost?
<--- Score

34. How sensitive must the Blockchain Solutions strategy be to cost?

<--- Score

35. How is performance measured?
<--- Score

36. What measurements are being captured?
<--- Score

37. What are the Blockchain Solutions investment costs?
<--- Score

38. What is the root cause(s) of the problem?
<--- Score

39. What could cause you to change course?
<--- Score

40. Are the measurements objective?
<--- Score

41. What users will be impacted?
<--- Score

42. What is your Blockchain Solutions quality cost segregation study?
<--- Score

43. What disadvantage does this cause for the user?
<--- Score

44. When should you bother with diagrams?
<--- Score

45. What are the estimated costs of proposed changes?

<--- Score

46. Are indirect costs charged to the Blockchain Solutions program?
<--- Score

47. Does management have the right priorities among projects?
<--- Score

48. What are the types and number of measures to use?
<--- Score

49. Which measures and indicators matter?
<--- Score

50. What are your customers expectations and measures?
<--- Score

51. What causes extra work or rework?
<--- Score

52. What can be used to verify compliance?
<--- Score

53. How long to keep data and how to manage retention costs?
<--- Score

54. How can you reduce costs?
<--- Score

55. What are the costs and benefits?
<--- Score

56. Which Blockchain Solutions impacts are significant?
<--- Score

57. What harm might be caused?
<--- Score

58. Are there measurements based on task performance?
<--- Score

59. What are your operating costs?
<--- Score

60. Has a cost center been established?
<--- Score

61. What are your primary costs, revenues, assets?
<--- Score

62. What relevant entities could be measured?
<--- Score

63. How will costs be allocated?
<--- Score

64. Is it possible to estimate the impact of unanticipated complexity such as wrong or failed assumptions, feedback, etcetera on proposed reforms?
<--- Score

65. How will you measure success?
<--- Score

66. How do you prevent mis-estimating cost?
<--- Score

67. When are costs are incurred?
<--- Score

68. What are allowable costs?
<--- Score

69. What would it cost to replace your technology?
<--- Score

70. What are hidden Blockchain Solutions quality costs?
<--- Score

71. How will you measure your Blockchain Solutions effectiveness?
<--- Score

72. What do you measure and why?
<--- Score

73. What causes innovation to fail or succeed in your organization?
<--- Score

74. How do you measure variability?
<--- Score

75. At what cost?
<--- Score

76. How do you aggregate measures across priorities?
<--- Score

77. Among the Blockchain Solutions product and service cost to be estimated, which is considered hardest to estimate?
<--- Score

78. What are the costs of reform?
<--- Score

79. Are you able to realize any cost savings?
<--- Score

80. What does your operating model cost?
<--- Score

81. Does a Blockchain Solutions quantification method exist?
<--- Score

82. Are you taking your company in the direction of better and revenue or cheaper and cost?
<--- Score

83. What are the strategic priorities for this year?
<--- Score

84. What are the current costs of the Blockchain Solutions process?
<--- Score

85. How are costs allocated?
<--- Score

86. Why do you expend time and effort to implement measurement, for whom?
<--- Score

87. What causes mismanagement?
<--- Score

88. Does the Blockchain Solutions task fit the client's priorities?
<--- Score

89. Have design-to-cost goals been established?
<--- Score

90. What are your key Blockchain Solutions organizational performance measures, including key short and longer-term financial measures?
<--- Score

91. Is there an opportunity to verify requirements?
<--- Score

92. How will effects be measured?
<--- Score

93. What drives O&M cost?
<--- Score

94. How can a Blockchain Solutions test verify your ideas or assumptions?
<--- Score

95. Are the units of measure consistent?
<--- Score

96. What do people want to verify?
<--- Score

97. What potential environmental factors impact the Blockchain Solutions effort?

<--- Score

98. Is the cost worth the Blockchain Solutions effort ?
<--- Score

99. Do you effectively measure and reward individual and team performance?
<--- Score

100. How will success or failure be measured?
<--- Score

101. Are the Blockchain Solutions benefits worth its costs?
<--- Score

102. What is the total cost related to deploying Blockchain Solutions, including any consulting or professional services?
<--- Score

103. How will your organization measure success?
<--- Score

104. What is measured? Why?
<--- Score

105. How can you measure the performance?
<--- Score

106. Will Blockchain Solutions have an impact on current business continuity, disaster recovery processes and/or infrastructure?
<--- Score

107. Do you aggressively reward and promote the

people who have the biggest impact on creating excellent Blockchain Solutions services/products?
<--- Score

108. Are supply costs steady or fluctuating?
<--- Score

109. Do you have a flow diagram of what happens?
<--- Score

110. Are missed Blockchain Solutions opportunities costing your organization money?
<--- Score

111. Which costs should be taken into account?
<--- Score

112. What are the costs of delaying Blockchain Solutions action?
<--- Score

113. How much does it cost?
<--- Score

114. Was a business case (cost/benefit) developed?
<--- Score

115. Are Blockchain Solutions vulnerabilities categorized and prioritized?
<--- Score

116. How can you manage cost down?
<--- Score

117. How do you measure efficient delivery of Blockchain Solutions services?

<--- Score

118. What are the costs?
<--- Score

119. Do you have an issue in getting priority?
<--- Score

120. How do you measure lifecycle phases?
<--- Score

121. Do you have any cost Blockchain Solutions limitation requirements?
<--- Score

122. How to cause the change?
<--- Score

123. What is the cost of rework?
<--- Score

124. How do you control the overall costs of your work processes?
<--- Score

125. How do your measurements capture actionable Blockchain Solutions information for use in exceeding your customers expectations and securing your customers engagement?
<--- Score

126. What details are required of the Blockchain Solutions cost structure?
<--- Score

127. Do the benefits outweigh the costs?

<--- Score

128. How do you quantify and qualify impacts?
<--- Score

129. What are the operational costs after Blockchain Solutions deployment?
<--- Score

130. How do you measure success?
<--- Score

Add up total points for this section:
_ _ _ _ _ = Total points for this section

Divided by: _ _ _ _ _ _ (number of statements answered) = _ _ _ _ _ _
Average score for this section

Transfer your score to the Blockchain Solutions Index at the beginning of the Self-Assessment.

CRITERION #4: ANALYZE:

INTENT: Analyze causes, assumptions and hypotheses.

In my belief, the answer to this question is clearly defined:

5 Strongly Agree

4 Agree

3 Neutral

2 Disagree

1 Strongly Disagree

1. What conclusions were drawn from the team's data collection and analysis? How did the team reach these conclusions?
<--- Score

2. Do your leaders quickly bounce back from setbacks?
<--- Score

3. What process improvements will be needed?

<--- Score

4. What internal processes need improvement?
<--- Score

5. Is there any way to speed up the process?
<--- Score

6. What quality tools were used to get through the analyze phase?
<--- Score

7. Who will gather what data?
<--- Score

8. What is your organizations process which leads to recognition of value generation?
<--- Score

9. What tools were used to generate the list of possible causes?
<--- Score

10. Were any designed experiments used to generate additional insight into the data analysis?
<--- Score

11. Do your employees have the opportunity to do what they do best everyday?
<--- Score

12. How do you promote understanding that opportunity for improvement is not criticism of the status quo, or the people who created the status quo?
<--- Score

13. What is the cost of poor quality as supported by the team's analysis?
<--- Score

14. What qualifies as competition?
<--- Score

15. What Blockchain Solutions metrics are outputs of the process?
<--- Score

16. Do staff qualifications match your project?
<--- Score

17. What systems/processes must you excel at?
<--- Score

18. Are your outputs consistent?
<--- Score

19. Who owns what data?
<--- Score

20. Is pre-qualification of suppliers carried out?
<--- Score

21. What did the team gain from developing a sub-process map?
<--- Score

22. How do you ensure that the Blockchain Solutions opportunity is realistic?
<--- Score

23. What tools were used to narrow the list of possible causes?

<--- Score

24. What successful thing are you doing today that may be blinding you to new growth opportunities?
<--- Score

25. Are all staff in core Blockchain Solutions subjects Highly Qualified?
<--- Score

26. What Blockchain Solutions data should be managed?
<--- Score

27. How does the organization define, manage, and improve its Blockchain Solutions processes?
<--- Score

28. What do you need to qualify?
<--- Score

29. How has the Blockchain Solutions data been gathered?
<--- Score

30. What other jobs or tasks affect the performance of the steps in the Blockchain Solutions process?
<--- Score

31. What methods do you use to gather Blockchain Solutions data?
<--- Score

32. Where is Blockchain Solutions data gathered?
<--- Score

33. What data is gathered?
<--- Score

34. How will corresponding data be collected?
<--- Score

35. How do you define collaboration and team output?
<--- Score

36. What is the output?
<--- Score

37. What data do you need to collect?
<--- Score

38. Do several people in different organizational units assist with the Blockchain Solutions process?
<--- Score

39. Think about the functions involved in your Blockchain Solutions project, what processes flow from these functions?
<--- Score

40. How do you measure the operational performance of your key work systems and processes, including productivity, cycle time, and other appropriate measures of process effectiveness, efficiency, and innovation?
<--- Score

41. How do mission and objectives affect the Blockchain Solutions processes of your organization?
<--- Score

42. Are you missing Blockchain Solutions opportunities?
<--- Score

43. When should a process be art not science?
<--- Score

44. What were the financial benefits resulting from any 'ground fruit or low-hanging fruit' (quick fixes)?
<--- Score

45. A compounding model resolution with available relevant data can often provide insight towards a solution methodology; which Blockchain Solutions models, tools and techniques are necessary?
<--- Score

46. How is Blockchain Solutions data gathered?
<--- Score

47. How can risk management be tied procedurally to process elements?
<--- Score

48. Are Blockchain Solutions changes recognized early enough to be approved through the regular process?
<--- Score

49. Do you understand your management processes today?
<--- Score

50. What are your current levels and trends in key Blockchain Solutions measures or indicators of product and process performance that are important to and directly serve your customers?

<--- Score

51. Is the suppliers process defined and controlled?
<--- Score

52. Is there a strict change management process?
<--- Score

53. Is the Blockchain Solutions process severely broken such that a re-design is necessary?
<--- Score

54. What are the revised rough estimates of the financial savings/opportunity for Blockchain Solutions improvements?
<--- Score

55. What qualifications are needed?
<--- Score

56. What are your best practices for minimizing Blockchain Solutions project risk, while demonstrating incremental value and quick wins throughout the Blockchain Solutions project lifecycle?
<--- Score

57. How much data can be collected in the given timeframe?
<--- Score

58. How is data used for program management and improvement?
<--- Score

59. Has data output been validated?
<--- Score

60. An organizationally feasible system request is one that considers the mission, goals and objectives of the organization, key questions are: is the Blockchain Solutions solution request practical and will it solve a problem or take advantage of an opportunity to achieve company goals?

<--- Score

61. Who will facilitate the team and process?

<--- Score

62. Do quality systems drive continuous improvement?

<--- Score

63. What will drive Blockchain Solutions change?

<--- Score

64. How will the data be checked for quality?

<--- Score

65. Were Pareto charts (or similar) used to portray the 'heavy hitters' (or key sources of variation)?

<--- Score

66. What information qualified as important?

<--- Score

67. What does the data say about the performance of the stakeholder process?

<--- Score

68. How do you identify specific Blockchain Solutions investment opportunities and emerging trends?

<--- Score

69. Who is involved with workflow mapping?
<--- Score

70. What are evaluation criteria for the output?
<--- Score

71. What training and qualifications will you need?
<--- Score

72. What are the disruptive Blockchain Solutions technologies that enable your organization to radically change your business processes?
<--- Score

73. Was a cause-and-effect diagram used to explore the different types of causes (or sources of variation)?
<--- Score

74. What are the processes for audit reporting and management?
<--- Score

75. How is the Blockchain Solutions Value Stream Mapping managed?
<--- Score

76. How will the Blockchain Solutions data be captured?
<--- Score

77. Is there an established change management process?
<--- Score

78. What Blockchain Solutions data will be collected?

<--- Score

79. What types of data do your Blockchain Solutions indicators require?
<--- Score

80. Were there any improvement opportunities identified from the process analysis?
<--- Score

81. What are your Blockchain Solutions processes?
<--- Score

82. Think about some of the processes you undertake within your organization, which do you own?
<--- Score

83. What controls do you have in place to protect data?
<--- Score

84. What are your outputs?
<--- Score

85. What are your current levels and trends in key measures or indicators of Blockchain Solutions product and process performance that are important to and directly serve your customers? How do these results compare with the performance of your competitors and other organizations with similar offerings?
<--- Score

86. What resources go in to get the desired output?
<--- Score

87. How do you implement and manage your work processes to ensure that they meet design requirements?
<--- Score

88. What are your key performance measures or indicators and in-process measures for the control and improvement of your Blockchain Solutions processes?
<--- Score

89. Is the final output clearly identified?
<--- Score

90. What other organizational variables, such as reward systems or communication systems, affect the performance of this Blockchain Solutions process?
<--- Score

91. Is the gap/opportunity displayed and communicated in financial terms?
<--- Score

92. What is the oversight process?
<--- Score

93. What is the Value Stream Mapping?
<--- Score

94. What is the complexity of the output produced?
<--- Score

95. What are the best opportunities for value improvement?
<--- Score

96. What qualifications are necessary?
<--- Score

97. Where is the data coming from to measure compliance?
<--- Score

98. Did any value-added analysis or 'lean thinking' take place to identify some of the gaps shown on the 'as is' process map?
<--- Score

99. Who is involved in the management review process?
<--- Score

100. Is data and process analysis, root cause analysis and quantifying the gap/opportunity in place?
<--- Score

101. Do you have the authority to produce the output?
<--- Score

102. Have any additional benefits been identified that will result from closing all or most of the gaps?
<--- Score

103. How are outputs preserved and protected?
<--- Score

104. Have the problem and goal statements been updated to reflect the additional knowledge gained from the analyze phase?
<--- Score

105. What are the Blockchain Solutions business drivers?
<--- Score

106. Did any additional data need to be collected?
<--- Score

107. Do your contracts/agreements contain data security obligations?
<--- Score

108. Record-keeping requirements flow from the records needed as inputs, outputs, controls and for transformation of a Blockchain Solutions process, are the records needed as inputs to the Blockchain Solutions process available?
<--- Score

109. Do you, as a leader, bounce back quickly from setbacks?
<--- Score

110. How is the data gathered?
<--- Score

111. How is the way you as the leader think and process information affecting your organizational culture?
<--- Score

112. How will the change process be managed?
<--- Score

113. What qualifications do Blockchain Solutions leaders need?
<--- Score

114. What are the Blockchain Solutions design outputs?

<--- Score

115. Which Blockchain Solutions data should be retained?

<--- Score

116. Are all team members qualified for all tasks?

<--- Score

117. What output to create?

<--- Score

118. How do your work systems and key work processes relate to and capitalize on your core competencies?

<--- Score

119. How do you use Blockchain Solutions data and information to support organizational decision making and innovation?

<--- Score

120. What are the necessary qualifications?

<--- Score

121. What Blockchain Solutions data do you gather or use now?

<--- Score

122. Is the performance gap determined?

<--- Score

123. Who qualifies to gain access to data?

<--- Score

124. What were the crucial 'moments of truth' on the process map?
<--- Score

125. Have you defined which data is gathered how?
<--- Score

126. How many input/output points does it require?
<--- Score

127. How difficult is it to qualify what Blockchain Solutions ROI is?
<--- Score

128. How was the detailed process map generated, verified, and validated?
<--- Score

129. Where can you get qualified talent today?
<--- Score

130. Has an output goal been set?
<--- Score

131. What is the Blockchain Solutions Driver?
<--- Score

132. Identify an operational issue in your organization, for example, could a particular task be done more quickly or more efficiently by Blockchain Solutions?
<--- Score

133. Was a detailed process map created to amplify critical steps of the 'as is' stakeholder process?

<--- Score

Add up total points for this section:
_ _ _ _ _   = Total points for this section

Divided by: _ _ _ _ _ _ _   (number of
statements answered) = _ _ _ _ _ _
Average score for this section

Transfer your score to the Blockchain
Solutions Index at the beginning of the
Self-Assessment.

CRITERION #5: IMPROVE:

INTENT: Develop a practical solution.
Innovate, establish and test the
solution and to measure the results.

In my belief, the answer to this
question is clearly defined:

5 Strongly Agree

4 Agree

3 Neutral

2 Disagree

1 Strongly Disagree

1. Risk factors: what are the characteristics of
Blockchain Solutions that make it risky?
<--- Score

2. How do you improve productivity?
<--- Score

3. At what point will vulnerability assessments be
performed once Blockchain Solutions is put into

production (e.g., ongoing Risk Management after implementation)?
<--- Score

4. What alternative responses are available to manage risk?
<--- Score

5. Have you achieved Blockchain Solutions improvements?
<--- Score

6. What criteria will you use to assess your Blockchain Solutions risks?
<--- Score

7. What should a proof of concept or pilot accomplish?
<--- Score

8. What strategies for Blockchain Solutions improvement are successful?
<--- Score

9. What attendant changes will need to be made to ensure that the solution is successful?
<--- Score

10. Is the Blockchain Solutions solution sustainable?
<--- Score

11. What is the implementation plan?
<--- Score

12. How do you link measurement and risk?
<--- Score

13. What tools were used to tap into the creativity and encourage 'outside the box' thinking?
<--- Score

14. When you map the key players in your own work and the types/domains of relationships with them, which relationships do you find easy and which challenging, and why?
<--- Score

15. To what extent does management recognize Blockchain Solutions as a tool to increase the results?
<--- Score

16. Are decisions made in a timely manner?
<--- Score

17. What is the magnitude of the improvements?
<--- Score

18. Do vendor agreements bring new compliance risk ?
<--- Score

19. Explorations of the frontiers of Blockchain Solutions will help you build influence, improve Blockchain Solutions, optimize decision making, and sustain change, what is your approach?
<--- Score

20. Can you identify any significant risks or exposures to Blockchain Solutions third- parties (vendors, service providers, alliance partners etc) that concern you?
<--- Score

21. What risks do you need to manage?
<--- Score

22. Do you need to do a usability evaluation?
<--- Score

23. How will you measure the results?
<--- Score

24. Were any criteria developed to assist the team in testing and evaluating potential solutions?
<--- Score

25. What does the 'should be' process map/design look like?
<--- Score

26. How do you improve Blockchain Solutions service perception, and satisfaction?
<--- Score

27. Why improve in the first place?
<--- Score

28. Who are the people involved in developing and implementing Blockchain Solutions?
<--- Score

29. What were the criteria for evaluating a Blockchain Solutions pilot?
<--- Score

30. Who are the Blockchain Solutions decision-makers?
<--- Score

31. Who controls the risk?
<--- Score

32. Who are the key stakeholders for the Blockchain Solutions evaluation?
<--- Score

33. Who should make the Blockchain Solutions decisions?
<--- Score

34. Are risk triggers captured?
<--- Score

35. How will you know when its improved?
<--- Score

36. Is the scope clearly documented?
<--- Score

37. What assumptions are made about the solution and approach?
<--- Score

38. Who will be responsible for documenting the Blockchain Solutions requirements in detail?
<--- Score

39. Are the most efficient solutions problem-specific?
<--- Score

40. Is the Blockchain Solutions risk managed?
<--- Score

41. What went well, what should change, what can improve?

<--- Score

42. What are the affordable Blockchain Solutions risks?
<--- Score

43. Is there a small-scale pilot for proposed improvement(s)? What conclusions were drawn from the outcomes of a pilot?
<--- Score

44. What resources are required for the improvement efforts?
<--- Score

45. Risk events: what are the things that could go wrong?
<--- Score

46. How do you deal with Blockchain Solutions risk?
<--- Score

47. What are the Blockchain Solutions security risks?
<--- Score

48. How do you go about comparing Blockchain Solutions approaches/solutions?
<--- Score

49. How can the phases of Blockchain Solutions development be identified?
<--- Score

50. What are the expected Blockchain Solutions results?
<--- Score

51. How do you measure progress and evaluate training effectiveness?
<--- Score

52. Are events managed to resolution?
<--- Score

53. Have you identified breakpoints and/or risk tolerances that will trigger broad consideration of a potential need for intervention or modification of strategy?
<--- Score

54. Was a Blockchain Solutions charter developed?
<--- Score

55. Are procedures documented for managing Blockchain Solutions risks?
<--- Score

56. What is the risk?
<--- Score

57. Is there a high likelihood that any recommendations will achieve their intended results?
<--- Score

58. How do the Blockchain Solutions results compare with the performance of your competitors and other organizations with similar offerings?
<--- Score

59. Was a pilot designed for the proposed solution(s)?
<--- Score

60. What is Blockchain Solutions's impact on utilizing

the best solution(s)?
<--- Score

61. What were the underlying assumptions on the cost-benefit analysis?
<--- Score

62. How do you keep improving Blockchain Solutions?
<--- Score

63. Is supporting Blockchain Solutions documentation required?
<--- Score

64. What needs improvement? Why?
<--- Score

65. What do you want to improve?
<--- Score

66. What area needs the greatest improvement?
<--- Score

67. How are policy decisions made and where?
<--- Score

68. Does the goal represent a desired result that can be measured?
<--- Score

69. Is there any other Blockchain Solutions solution?
<--- Score

70. How will you recognize and celebrate results?
<--- Score

71. Where do you need Blockchain Solutions improvement?
<--- Score

72. Which of the recognised risks out of all risks can be most likely transferred?
<--- Score

73. Is the measure of success for Blockchain Solutions understandable to a variety of people?
<--- Score

74. How do you improve your likelihood of success ?
<--- Score

75. What are your current levels and trends in key measures or indicators of workforce and leader development?
<--- Score

76. How can you improve Blockchain Solutions?
<--- Score

77. Who manages Blockchain Solutions risk?
<--- Score

78. Who manages supplier risk management in your organization?
<--- Score

79. How do you measure risk?
<--- Score

80. Who are the Blockchain Solutions decision makers?
<--- Score

81. How do you decide how much to remunerate an employee?
<--- Score

82. What actually has to improve and by how much?
<--- Score

83. What tools do you use once you have decided on a Blockchain Solutions strategy and more importantly how do you choose?
<--- Score

84. How does your organization evaluate strategic Blockchain Solutions success?
<--- Score

85. Who do you report Blockchain Solutions results to?
<--- Score

86. How are Blockchain Solutions risks managed?
<--- Score

87. Are you assessing Blockchain Solutions and risk?
<--- Score

88. What are the concrete Blockchain Solutions results?
<--- Score

89. How do you measure improved Blockchain Solutions service perception, and satisfaction?
<--- Score

90. When is it too early/too late to develop

blockchain solutions?
<--- Score

91. What can you do to improve?
<--- Score

92. Are the risks fully understood, reasonable and manageable?
<--- Score

93. How can you better manage risk?
<--- Score

94. Is the Blockchain Solutions documentation thorough?
<--- Score

95. How do you mitigate Blockchain Solutions risk?
<--- Score

96. If you could go back in time five years, what decision would you make differently? What is your best guess as to what decision you're making today you might regret five years from now?
<--- Score

97. What is the team's contingency plan for potential problems occurring in implementation?
<--- Score

98. How is knowledge sharing about risk management improved?
<--- Score

99. What improvements have been achieved?
<--- Score

100. What to do with the results or outcomes of measurements?
<--- Score

101. How does the team improve its work?
<--- Score

102. Do you have the optimal project management team structure?
<--- Score

103. Do you combine technical expertise with business knowledge and Blockchain Solutions Key topics include lifecycles, development approaches, requirements and how to make a business case?
<--- Score

104. Are risk management tasks balanced centrally and locally?
<--- Score

105. Do you cover the five essential competencies: Communication, Collaboration,Innovation, Adaptability, and Leadership that improve an organizations ability to leverage the new Blockchain Solutions in a volatile global economy?
<--- Score

106. Is any Blockchain Solutions documentation required?
<--- Score

107. How do you define the solutions' scope?
<--- Score

108. Is the solution technically practical?
<--- Score

109. Can you integrate quality management and risk management?
<--- Score

110. Is risk periodically assessed?
<--- Score

111. How can skill-level changes improve Blockchain Solutions?
<--- Score

112. For decision problems, how do you develop a decision statement?
<--- Score

113. What lessons, if any, from a pilot were incorporated into the design of the full-scale solution?
<--- Score

114. How is continuous improvement applied to risk management?
<--- Score

115. Which Blockchain Solutions solution is appropriate?
<--- Score

116. What communications are necessary to support the implementation of the solution?
<--- Score

117. How can you improve performance?
<--- Score

118. Who will be responsible for making the decisions to include or exclude requested changes once Blockchain Solutions is underway?
<--- Score

119. Can the solution be designed and implemented within an acceptable time period?
<--- Score

120. In the past few months, what is the smallest change you have made that has had the biggest positive result? What was it about that small change that produced the large return?
<--- Score

121. What Blockchain Solutions improvements can be made?
<--- Score

122. Where do the Blockchain Solutions decisions reside?
<--- Score

123. How do you manage Blockchain Solutions risk?
<--- Score

124. Who will be using the results of the measurement activities?
<--- Score

125. Who controls key decisions that will be made?
<--- Score

126. What tools were used to evaluate the potential solutions?

<--- Score

127. How will you know that you have improved?
<--- Score

128. Risk Identification: What are the possible
risk events your organization faces in relation to
Blockchain Solutions?
<--- Score

129. What are the implications of the one critical
Blockchain Solutions decision 10 minutes, 10 months,
and 10 years from now?
<--- Score

130. Is Blockchain Solutions documentation
maintained?
<--- Score

131. Are the key business and technology risks being
managed?
<--- Score

132. What tools were most useful during the improve
phase?
<--- Score

133. For estimation problems, how do you develop an
estimation statement?
<--- Score

134. Will the controls trigger any other risks?
<--- Score

135. What is Blockchain Solutions risk?
<--- Score

136. Do those selected for the Blockchain Solutions team have a good general understanding of what Blockchain Solutions is all about?
<--- Score

137. What error proofing will be done to address some of the discrepancies observed in the 'as is' process?
<--- Score

138. What is the Blockchain Solutions's sustainability risk?
<--- Score

139. How risky is your organization?
<--- Score

Add up total points for this section:
_ _ _ _ _ = Total points for this section

Divided by: _ _ _ _ _ _ (number of statements answered) = _ _ _ _ _ _
Average score for this section

Transfer your score to the Blockchain Solutions Index at the beginning of the Self-Assessment.

CRITERION #6: CONTROL:

INTENT: Implement the practical solution. Maintain the performance and correct possible complications.

In my belief, the answer to this question is clearly defined:

5 Strongly Agree

4 Agree

3 Neutral

2 Disagree

1 Strongly Disagree

1. What are the known security controls?
<--- Score

2. Have new or revised work instructions resulted?
<--- Score

3. Are the Blockchain Solutions standards challenging?
<--- Score

4. Against what alternative is success being measured?
<--- Score

5. What key inputs and outputs are being measured on an ongoing basis?
<--- Score

6. Who has control over resources?
<--- Score

7. Is new knowledge gained imbedded in the response plan?
<--- Score

8. Has the Blockchain Solutions value of standards been quantified?
<--- Score

9. Does the response plan contain a definite closed loop continual improvement scheme (e.g., plan-do-check-act)?
<--- Score

10. How can you best use all of your knowledge repositories to enhance learning and sharing?
<--- Score

11. How might the group capture best practices and lessons learned so as to leverage improvements?
<--- Score

12. What are the critical parameters to watch?
<--- Score

13. Has the improved process and its steps been standardized?
<--- Score

14. What are you attempting to measure/monitor?
<--- Score

15. How is Blockchain Solutions project cost planned, managed, monitored?
<--- Score

16. Act/Adjust: What Do you Need to Do Differently?
<--- Score

17. Can support from partners be adjusted?
<--- Score

18. Is reporting being used or needed?
<--- Score

19. Implementation Planning: is a pilot needed to test the changes before a full roll out occurs?
<--- Score

20. What quality tools were useful in the control phase?
<--- Score

21. Is there a control plan in place for sustaining improvements (short and long-term)?
<--- Score

22. You may have created your quality measures at a time when you lacked resources, technology wasn't up to the required standard, or low service levels were the industry norm. Have those circumstances

changed?
<--- Score

23. Does job training on the documented procedures need to be part of the process team's education and training?
<--- Score

24. What adjustments to the strategies are needed?
<--- Score

25. Are you measuring, monitoring and predicting Blockchain Solutions activities to optimize operations and profitability, and enhancing outcomes?
<--- Score

26. Are suggested corrective/restorative actions indicated on the response plan for known causes to problems that might surface?
<--- Score

27. What do you measure to verify effectiveness gains?
<--- Score

28. How do senior leaders actions reflect a commitment to the organizations Blockchain Solutions values?
<--- Score

29. How likely is the current Blockchain Solutions plan to come in on schedule or on budget?
<--- Score

30. How will you measure your QA plan's effectiveness?

<--- Score

31. Is there an action plan in case of emergencies?
<--- Score

32. How widespread is its use?
<--- Score

33. Will existing staff require re-training, for example, to learn new business processes?
<--- Score

34. Does the Blockchain Solutions performance meet the customer's requirements?
<--- Score

35. Does Blockchain Solutions appropriately measure and monitor risk?
<--- Score

36. What is the standard for acceptable Blockchain Solutions performance?
<--- Score

37. Is the Blockchain Solutions test/monitoring cost justified?
<--- Score

38. How will input, process, and output variables be checked to detect for sub-optimal conditions?
<--- Score

39. How will the process owner verify improvement in present and future sigma levels, process capabilities?
<--- Score

40. What do you stand for--and what are you against?
<--- Score

41. What is the best design framework for Blockchain Solutions organization now that, in a post industrial-age if the top-down, command and control model is no longer relevant?
<--- Score

42. Are new process steps, standards, and documentation ingrained into normal operations?
<--- Score

43. How will new or emerging customer needs/requirements be checked/communicated to orient the process toward meeting the new specifications and continually reducing variation?
<--- Score

44. Are there documented procedures?
<--- Score

45. Do you monitor the effectiveness of your Blockchain Solutions activities?
<--- Score

46. What is the recommended frequency of auditing?
<--- Score

47. Are the planned controls in place?
<--- Score

48. Is knowledge gained on process shared and institutionalized?
<--- Score

49. Do the viable solutions scale to future needs?
<--- Score

50. How do you plan for the cost of succession?
<--- Score

51. How do you select, collect, align, and integrate Blockchain Solutions data and information for tracking daily operations and overall organizational performance, including progress relative to strategic objectives and action plans?
<--- Score

52. Are operating procedures consistent?
<--- Score

53. Who will be in control?
<--- Score

54. Who controls critical resources?
<--- Score

55. How do you monitor usage and cost?
<--- Score

56. What should the next improvement project be that is related to Blockchain Solutions?
<--- Score

57. How do controls support value?
<--- Score

58. How do you plan on providing proper recognition and disclosure of supporting companies?
<--- Score

59. What other systems, operations, processes, and infrastructures (hiring practices, staffing, training, incentives/rewards, metrics/dashboards/scorecards, etc.) need updates, additions, changes, or deletions in order to facilitate knowledge transfer and improvements?

<--- Score

60. Is there a Blockchain Solutions Communication plan covering who needs to get what information when?

<--- Score

61. Is there a transfer of ownership and knowledge to process owner and process team tasked with the responsibilities.

<--- Score

62. What would the competitive advantage be for your organization effectively using blockchain solutions at scale in the future?

<--- Score

63. Is a response plan in place for when the input, process, or output measures indicate an 'out-of-control' condition?

<--- Score

64. Will the team be available to assist members in planning investigations?

<--- Score

65. Is there a standardized process?

<--- Score

66. Is there documentation that will support the

successful operation of the improvement?
<--- Score

67. What is your plan to assess your security risks?
<--- Score

68. Will any special training be provided for results interpretation?
<--- Score

69. What should you measure to verify efficiency gains?
<--- Score

70. What are customers monitoring?
<--- Score

71. What is the control/monitoring plan?
<--- Score

72. Where do ideas that reach policy makers and planners as proposals for Blockchain Solutions strengthening and reform actually originate?
<--- Score

73. Is there a recommended audit plan for routine surveillance inspections of Blockchain Solutions's gains?
<--- Score

74. What Blockchain Solutions standards are applicable?
<--- Score

75. Can you adapt and adjust to changing Blockchain Solutions situations?

<--- Score

76. What other areas of the group might benefit from the Blockchain Solutions team's improvements, knowledge, and learning?
<--- Score

77. Are the planned controls working?
<--- Score

78. How do you establish and deploy modified action plans if circumstances require a shift in plans and rapid execution of new plans?
<--- Score

79. Who is the Blockchain Solutions process owner?
<--- Score

80. How will the day-to-day responsibilities for monitoring and continual improvement be transferred from the improvement team to the process owner?
<--- Score

81. Will your goals reflect your program budget?
<--- Score

82. How do you encourage people to take control and responsibility?
<--- Score

83. Is a response plan established and deployed?
<--- Score

84. What do your reports reflect?
<--- Score

85. Are documented procedures clear and easy to follow for the operators?
<--- Score

86. Do you monitor the Blockchain Solutions decisions made and fine tune them as they evolve?
<--- Score

87. How will the process owner and team be able to hold the gains?
<--- Score

88. Who is going to spread your message?
<--- Score

89. Is there a documented and implemented monitoring plan?
<--- Score

90. What can you control?
<--- Score

91. How will Blockchain Solutions decisions be made and monitored?
<--- Score

92. Are controls in place and consistently applied?
<--- Score

93. How will report readings be checked to effectively monitor performance?
<--- Score

94. Does a troubleshooting guide exist or is it needed?
<--- Score

95. What are the key elements of your Blockchain Solutions performance improvement system, including your evaluation, organizational learning, and innovation processes?
<--- Score

96. How do your controls stack up?
<--- Score

97. In the case of a Blockchain Solutions project, the criteria for the audit derive from implementation objectives, an audit of a Blockchain Solutions project involves assessing whether the recommendations outlined for implementation have been met, can you track that any Blockchain Solutions project is implemented as planned, and is it working?
<--- Score

98. What are your results for key measures or indicators of the accomplishment of your Blockchain Solutions strategy and action plans, including building and strengthening core competencies?
<--- Score

Add up total points for this section:
_____ = Total points for this section

Divided by: _____ (number of
statements answered) = _____
Average score for this section

Transfer your score to the Blockchain Solutions Index at the beginning of the Self-Assessment.

CRITERION #7: SUSTAIN:

INTENT: Retain the benefits.

In my belief, the answer to this question is clearly defined:

5 Strongly Agree

4 Agree

3 Neutral

2 Disagree

1 Strongly Disagree

1. What happens at your organization when people fail?
<--- Score

2. What are the key enablers to make this Blockchain Solutions move?
<--- Score

3. What is the craziest thing you can do?
<--- Score

4. How do you ensure that implementations of Blockchain Solutions products are done in a way that ensures safety?
<--- Score

5. Who do we want your customers to become?
<--- Score

6. How do senior leaders deploy your organizations vision and values through your leadership system, to the workforce, to key suppliers and partners, and to customers and other stakeholders, as appropriate?
<--- Score

7. Why do and why don't your customers like your organization?
<--- Score

8. Is maximizing Blockchain Solutions protection the same as minimizing Blockchain Solutions loss?
<--- Score

9. Is a Blockchain Solutions breakthrough on the horizon?
<--- Score

10. Are you / should you be revolutionary or evolutionary?
<--- Score

11. Would you rather sell to knowledgeable and informed customers or to uninformed customers?
<--- Score

12. What are the gaps in your knowledge and experience?

<--- Score

13. How do you manage Blockchain Solutions Knowledge Management (KM)?
<--- Score

14. What would have to be true for the option on the table to be the best possible choice?
<--- Score

15. If you had to rebuild your organization without any traditional competitive advantages (i.e., no killer technology, promising research, innovative product/ service delivery model, etcetera), how would your people have to approach their work and collaborate together in order to create the necessary conditions for success?
<--- Score

16. What is something you believe that nearly no one agrees with you on?
<--- Score

17. If you find that you havent accomplished one of the goals for one of the steps of the Blockchain Solutions strategy, what will you do to fix it?
<--- Score

18. Has implementation been effective in reaching specified objectives so far?
<--- Score

19. What stupid rule would you most like to kill?
<--- Score

20. What is effective Blockchain Solutions?

<--- Score

21. How do you assess the Blockchain Solutions pitfalls that are inherent in implementing it?
<--- Score

22. What is the overall business strategy?
<--- Score

23. Ask yourself: how would you do this work if you only had one staff member to do it?
<--- Score

24. Can you do all this work?
<--- Score

25. What is your Blockchain Solutions strategy?
<--- Score

26. If you were responsible for initiating and implementing major changes in your organization, what steps might you take to ensure acceptance of those changes?
<--- Score

27. Are the assumptions believable and achievable?
<--- Score

28. How will you motivate the stakeholders with the least vested interest?
<--- Score

29. Who have you, as a company, historically been when you've been at your best?
<--- Score

30. How do you keep records, of what?
<--- Score

31. Will there be any necessary staff changes (redundancies or new hires)?
<--- Score

32. What should you stop doing?
<--- Score

33. How do you maintain Blockchain Solutions's Integrity?
<--- Score

34. How do you lead with Blockchain Solutions in mind?
<--- Score

35. How do customers see your organization?
<--- Score

36. How will you know that the Blockchain Solutions project has been successful?
<--- Score

37. Who, on the executive team or the board, has spoken to a customer recently?
<--- Score

38. If your company went out of business tomorrow, would anyone who doesn't get a paycheck here care?
<--- Score

39. Which individuals, teams or departments will be involved in Blockchain Solutions?
<--- Score

40. Why is Blockchain Solutions important for you now?

<--- Score

41. If your customer were your grandmother, would you tell her to buy what you're selling?

<--- Score

42. How do you transition from the baseline to the target?

<--- Score

43. Think of your Blockchain Solutions project, what are the main functions?

<--- Score

44. What is your BATNA (best alternative to a negotiated agreement)?

<--- Score

45. Why should people listen to you?

<--- Score

46. Do you think you know, or do you know you know ?

<--- Score

47. Political -is anyone trying to undermine this project?

<--- Score

48. Operational - will it work?

<--- Score

49. Who are your customers?

<--- Score

50. Will it be accepted by users?
<--- Score

51. What are the challenges?
<--- Score

52. Marketing budgets are tighter, consumers are more skeptical, and social media has changed forever the way we talk about Blockchain Solutions, how do you gain traction?
<--- Score

53. Are the criteria for selecting recommendations stated?
<--- Score

54. Who will determine interim and final deadlines?
<--- Score

55. Why not do Blockchain Solutions?
<--- Score

56. What is the estimated value of the project?
<--- Score

57. Who is responsible for ensuring appropriate resources (time, people and money) are allocated to Blockchain Solutions?
<--- Score

58. How is implementation research currently incorporated into each of your goals?
<--- Score

59. What does your signature ensure?
<--- Score

60. What is an unauthorized commitment?
<--- Score

61. Whom among your colleagues do you trust, and for what?
<--- Score

62. What have been your experiences in defining long range Blockchain Solutions goals?
<--- Score

63. Who is the main stakeholder, with ultimate responsibility for driving Blockchain Solutions forward?
<--- Score

64. What Blockchain Solutions modifications can you make work for you?
<--- Score

65. Who uses your product in ways you never expected?
<--- Score

66. Do you have the right capabilities and capacities?
<--- Score

67. Is there a work around that you can use?
<--- Score

68. If you had to leave your organization for a year and the only communication you could have with employees/colleagues was a single paragraph, what

would you write?
<--- Score

69. What you are going to do to affect the numbers?
<--- Score

70. How can you become the company that would put you out of business?
<--- Score

71. Where can you break convention?
<--- Score

72. How do you deal with Blockchain Solutions changes?
<--- Score

73. Who are four people whose careers you have enhanced?
<--- Score

74. What are the short and long-term Blockchain Solutions goals?
<--- Score

75. What is your competitive advantage?
<--- Score

76. What is it like to work for you?
<--- Score

77. If you got fired and a new hire took your place, what would she do different?
<--- Score

78. Is a Blockchain Solutions team work effort in

place?
<--- Score

79. Can the schedule be done in the given time?
<--- Score

80. Are there any activities that you can take off your to do list?
<--- Score

81. Which functions and people interact with the supplier and or customer?
<--- Score

82. Have new benefits been realized?
<--- Score

83. Do you know what you are doing? And who do you call if you don't?
<--- Score

84. Is it economical; do you have the time and money?
<--- Score

85. What are the top 3 things at the forefront of your Blockchain Solutions agendas for the next 3 years?
<--- Score

86. Who else should you help?
<--- Score

87. What role does communication play in the success or failure of a Blockchain Solutions project?
<--- Score

88. What is the range of capabilities?

<--- Score

89. What threat is Blockchain Solutions addressing?
<--- Score

90. What happens when a new employee joins the organization?
<--- Score

91. What is the kind of project structure that would be appropriate for your Blockchain Solutions project, should it be formal and complex, or can it be less formal and relatively simple?
<--- Score

92. Do you say no to customers for no reason?
<--- Score

93. What is the purpose of Blockchain Solutions in relation to the mission?
<--- Score

94. Are you paying enough attention to the partners your company depends on to succeed?
<--- Score

95. What are the rules and assumptions your industry operates under? What if the opposite were true?
<--- Score

96. Who is responsible for Blockchain Solutions?
<--- Score

97. What are the usability implications of Blockchain Solutions actions?
<--- Score

98. Are all key stakeholders present at all Structured Walkthroughs?
<--- Score

99. What is the recommended frequency of auditing?
<--- Score

100. What management system can you use to leverage the Blockchain Solutions experience, ideas, and concerns of the people closest to the work to be done?
<--- Score

101. Are you relevant? Will you be relevant five years from now? Ten?
<--- Score

102. What are you challenging?
<--- Score

103. What projects are going on in the organization today, and what resources are those projects using from the resource pools?
<--- Score

104. How do you know if you are successful?
<--- Score

105. What is a feasible sequencing of reform initiatives over time?
<--- Score

106. In retrospect, of the projects that you pulled the plug on, what percent do you wish had been allowed to keep going, and what percent do you wish had

ended earlier?

<--- Score

107. How do you keep the momentum going?

<--- Score

108. How do you govern and fulfill your societal responsibilities?

<--- Score

109. Are you changing as fast as the world around you?

<--- Score

110. How do you accomplish your long range Blockchain Solutions goals?

<--- Score

111. Who do you want your customers to become?

<--- Score

112. How much contingency will be available in the budget?

<--- Score

113. Is Blockchain Solutions realistic, or are you setting yourself up for failure?

<--- Score

114. Whose voice (department, ethnic group, women, older workers, etc) might you have missed hearing from in your company, and how might you amplify this voice to create positive momentum for your business?

<--- Score

115. How do you go about securing Blockchain Solutions?

<--- Score

116. How do you listen to customers to obtain actionable information?

<--- Score

117. What are the business goals Blockchain Solutions is aiming to achieve?

<--- Score

118. Which Blockchain Solutions goals are the most important?

<--- Score

119. Is there any existing Blockchain Solutions governance structure?

<--- Score

120. Can you break it down?

<--- Score

121. What are the long-term Blockchain Solutions goals?

<--- Score

122. If there were zero limitations, what would you do differently?

<--- Score

123. Instead of going to current contacts for new ideas, what if you reconnected with dormant contacts--the people you used to know? If you were going reactivate a dormant tie, who would it be?

<--- Score

124. At what moment would you think; Will I get fired?
<--- Score

125. What is the funding source for this project?
<--- Score

126. What may be the consequences for the performance of an organization if all stakeholders are not consulted regarding Blockchain Solutions?
<--- Score

127. Who are the key stakeholders?
<--- Score

128. What did you miss in the interview for the worst hire you ever made?
<--- Score

129. Is Blockchain Solutions dependent on the successful delivery of a current project?
<--- Score

130. How do you track customer value, profitability or financial return, organizational success, and sustainability?
<--- Score

131. Who will be responsible for deciding whether Blockchain Solutions goes ahead or not after the initial investigations?
<--- Score

132. How do you provide a safe environment -physically and emotionally?
<--- Score

133. In the past year, what have you done (or could you have done) to increase the accurate perception of your company/brand as ethical and honest?
<--- Score

134. Why will customers want to buy your organizations products/services?
<--- Score

135. Do you have an implicit bias for capital investments over people investments?
<--- Score

136. How do you proactively clarify deliverables and Blockchain Solutions quality expectations?
<--- Score

137. Why should you adopt a Blockchain Solutions framework?
<--- Score

138. If you do not follow, then how to lead?
<--- Score

139. Is there any reason to believe the opposite of my current belief?
<--- Score

140. Which models, tools and techniques are necessary?
<--- Score

141. Is your basic point _____ or _____?
<--- Score

142. What one word do you want to own in the minds of your customers, employees, and partners?
<--- Score

143. What are the essentials of internal Blockchain Solutions management?
<--- Score

144. What is the big Blockchain Solutions idea?
<--- Score

145. Are you maintaining a past–present–future perspective throughout the Blockchain Solutions discussion?
<--- Score

146. Do you have enough freaky customers in your portfolio pushing you to the limit day in and day out?
<--- Score

147. What are the success criteria that will indicate that Blockchain Solutions objectives have been met and the benefits delivered?
<--- Score

148. Do you see more potential in people than they do in themselves?
<--- Score

149. Is the impact that Blockchain Solutions has shown?
<--- Score

150. How do you cross-sell and up-sell your Blockchain Solutions success?
<--- Score

151. How do you stay inspired?
<--- Score

152. Are you using a design thinking approach and integrating Innovation, Blockchain Solutions Experience, and Brand Value?
<--- Score

153. What are strategies for increasing support and reducing opposition?
<--- Score

154. Do you know who is a friend or a foe?
<--- Score

155. What are internal and external Blockchain Solutions relations?
<--- Score

156. Is your strategy driving your strategy? Or is the way in which you allocate resources driving your strategy?
<--- Score

157. What could happen if you do not do it?
<--- Score

158. Are new benefits received and understood?
<--- Score

159. Do Blockchain Solutions rules make a reasonable demand on a users capabilities?
<--- Score

160. How will you ensure you get what you expected?

<--- Score

161. How do you engage the workforce, in addition to satisfying them?
<--- Score

162. How do you foster the skills, knowledge, talents, attributes, and characteristics you want to have?
<--- Score

163. What do we do when new problems arise?
<--- Score

164. What goals did you miss?
<--- Score

165. Do you have the right people on the bus?
<--- Score

166. Why is it important to have senior management support for a Blockchain Solutions project?
<--- Score

167. Who will provide the final approval of Blockchain Solutions deliverables?
<--- Score

168. How do you make it meaningful in connecting Blockchain Solutions with what users do day-to-day?
<--- Score

169. How long will it take to change?
<--- Score

170. Are you satisfied with your current role? If not, what is missing from it?

<--- Score

171. What is your formula for success in Blockchain Solutions ?
<--- Score

172. What are specific Blockchain Solutions rules to follow?
<--- Score

173. How do you set Blockchain Solutions stretch targets and how do you get people to not only participate in setting these stretch targets but also that they strive to achieve these?
<--- Score

174. What must you excel at?
<--- Score

175. If you weren't already in this business, would you enter it today? And if not, what are you going to do about it?
<--- Score

176. To whom do you add value?
<--- Score

177. What are the barriers to increased Blockchain Solutions production?
<--- Score

178. What trouble can you get into?
<--- Score

179. How will you insure seamless interoperability of Blockchain Solutions moving forward?

<--- Score

180. Are your responses positive or negative?
<--- Score

181. What are current Blockchain Solutions paradigms?
<--- Score

182. What have you done to protect your business from competitive encroachment?
<--- Score

183. What are your personal philosophies regarding Blockchain Solutions and how do they influence your work?
<--- Score

184. What relationships among Blockchain Solutions trends do you perceive?
<--- Score

185. Who do you think the world wants your organization to be?
<--- Score

186. How do you foster innovation?
<--- Score

187. What was the last experiment you ran?
<--- Score

188. Have benefits been optimized with all key stakeholders?
<--- Score

189. How are you doing compared to your industry?
<--- Score

190. What information is critical to your organization that your executives are ignoring?
<--- Score

191. Are assumptions made in Blockchain Solutions stated explicitly?
<--- Score

192. What are your most important goals for the strategic Blockchain Solutions objectives?
<--- Score

193. Were lessons learned captured and communicated?
<--- Score

194. What knowledge, skills and characteristics mark a good Blockchain Solutions project manager?
<--- Score

195. Do you think Blockchain Solutions accomplishes the goals you expect it to accomplish?
<--- Score

196. What Blockchain Solutions skills are most important?
<--- Score

197. How does Blockchain Solutions integrate with other stakeholder initiatives?
<--- Score

198. What will be the consequences to the

stakeholder (financial, reputation etc) if Blockchain Solutions does not go ahead or fails to deliver the objectives?

<--- Score

199. How can you incorporate support to ensure safe and effective use of Blockchain Solutions into the services that you provide?

<--- Score

200. How can you negotiate Blockchain Solutions successfully with a stubborn boss, an irate client, or a deceitful coworker?

<--- Score

201. Who will manage the integration of tools?

<--- Score

202. What counts that you are not counting?

<--- Score

203. What happens if you do not have enough funding?

<--- Score

204. What are the potential basics of Blockchain Solutions fraud?

<--- Score

205. Do you have past Blockchain Solutions successes?

<--- Score

206. How do you create buy-in?

<--- Score

207. How much does Blockchain Solutions help?
<--- Score

208. Did your employees make progress today?
<--- Score

209. Is the Blockchain Solutions organization completing tasks effectively and efficiently?
<--- Score

Add up total points for this section:
_ _ _ _ _ = Total points for this section

Divided by: _ _ _ _ _ _ (number of statements answered) = _ _ _ _ _ _
Average score for this section

Transfer your score to the Blockchain Solutions Index at the beginning of the Self-Assessment.

Blockchain Solutions and Managing Projects, Criteria for Project Managers:

1.0 Initiating Process Group: Blockchain Solutions

1. Just how important is your work to the overall success of the Blockchain Solutions project?

2. Where must it be done?

3. How to control and approve each phase?

4. At which cmmi level are software processes documented, standardized, and integrated into a standard to-be practiced process for your organization?

5. What are the pressing issues of the hour?

6. Information sharing?

7. How will you do it?

8. If action is called for, what form should it take?

9. How well did you do?

10. What communication items need improvement?

11. Who does what?

12. How can you make your needs known?

13. First of all, should any action be taken?

14. Were decisions made in a timely manner?

15. Who is involved in each phase?

16. If the risk event occurs, what will you do?

17. What will you do to minimize the impact should a risk event occur?

18. Will the Blockchain Solutions project meet the client requirements, and will it achieve the business success criteria that justified doing the Blockchain Solutions project in the first place?

19. Did the Blockchain Solutions project team have the right skills?

20. The Blockchain Solutions project you are managing has nine stakeholders. How many channel of communications are there between corresponding stakeholders?

1.1 Project Charter: Blockchain Solutions

21. Why Outsource?

22. How much?

23. Pop quiz – which are the same inputs as in the Blockchain Solutions project charter?

24. Does the Blockchain Solutions project need to consider any special capacity or capability issues?

25. Success determination factors: how will the success of the Blockchain Solutions project be determined from the customers perspective?

26. What are some examples of a business case?

27. Are you building in-house ?

28. Assumptions and constraints: what assumptions were made in defining the Blockchain Solutions project?

29. How are Blockchain Solutions projects different from operations?

30. When do you use a Blockchain Solutions project Charter?

31. Why use a Blockchain Solutions project charter?

32. Who is the sponsor?

33. How high should you set your goals?

34. Avoid costs, improve service, and/ or comply with a mandate?

35. What are you striving to accomplish (measurable goal(s))?

36. Who is the Blockchain Solutions project Manager?

37. Customer benefits: what customer requirements does this Blockchain Solutions project address?

38. Who are the stakeholders?

39. If finished, on what date did it finish?

40. When is a charter needed?

1.2 Stakeholder Register: Blockchain Solutions

41. How should employers make voices heard?

42. How will reports be created?

43. Is your organization ready for change?

44. How big is the gap?

45. Who wants to talk about Security?

46. What opportunities exist to provide communications?

47. What & Why?

48. How much influence do they have on the Blockchain Solutions project?

49. What are the major Blockchain Solutions project milestones requiring communications or providing communications opportunities?

50. What is the power of the stakeholder?

51. Who is managing stakeholder engagement?

1.3 Stakeholder Analysis Matrix: Blockchain Solutions

52. Who will promote/support the Blockchain Solutions project, provided that they are involved?

53. Where are mitigation costs factored in?

54. What do people from other organizations see as your organizations weaknesses?

55. What obstacles does your organization face?

56. Financial reserves, likely returns?

57. Timescales, deadlines and pressures?

58. Are there different rules or organizational models for men and women?

59. Could any of your organizations weaknesses seriously threaten development?

60. What is relationship with the Blockchain Solutions project?

61. Who can contribute financial or technical resources towards the work?

62. What do you Evaluate?

63. New USPs?

64. Are you working on the right risks?

65. Processes and systems, etc?

66. What is the relationship among stakeholders?

67. Competitive advantages?

68. Which conditions out of the control of the management are crucial for the achievement of the outputs?

69. How does the Blockchain Solutions project involve consultations or collaboration with other organizations?

70. Information and research?

71. Are there two or three that rise to the top, and a couple that are sliding to the bottom?

2.0 Planning Process Group: Blockchain Solutions

72. How well did the chosen processes fit the needs of the Blockchain Solutions project?

73. To what extent do the intervention objectives and strategies of the Blockchain Solutions project respond to your organizations plans?

74. Will you be replaced?

75. How well do the team follow the chosen processes?

76. Are work methodologies, financial instruments, etc. shared among departments, organizations and Blockchain Solutions projects?

77. To what extent is the program helping to influence your organizations policy framework?

78. How will you know you did it?

79. If you are late, will anybody notice?

80. Have more efficient (sensitive) and appropriate measures been adopted to respond to the political and socio-cultural problems identified?

81. Why is it important to determine activity sequencing on Blockchain Solutions projects?

82. What is the critical path for this Blockchain Solutions project, and what is the duration of the critical path?

83. Did the program design/ implementation strategy adequately address the planning stage necessary to set up structures, hire staff etc.?

84. What do you need to do?

85. Is the Blockchain Solutions project supported by national and/or local organizations?

86. Who are the Blockchain Solutions project stakeholders?

87. The Blockchain Solutions project charter is created in which Blockchain Solutions project management process group?

88. Mitigate. what will you do to minimize the impact should a risk event occur?

89. In which Blockchain Solutions project management process group is the detailed Blockchain Solutions project budget created?

2.1 Project Management Plan: Blockchain Solutions

90. Does the selected plan protect privacy?

91. Who manages integration?

92. What is the business need?

93. What would you do differently?

94. Is mitigation authorized or recommended?

95. What is Blockchain Solutions project scope management?

96. What are the assumptions?

97. What did not work so well?

98. Is the budget realistic?

99. Does the implementation plan have an appropriate division of responsibilities?

100. When is a Blockchain Solutions project management plan created?

101. Will you add a schedule and diagram?

102. Are there any Client staffing expectations?

103. Is the appropriate plan selected based on your

organizations objectives and evaluation criteria expressed in Principles and Guidelines policies?

104. If the Blockchain Solutions project management plan is a comprehensive document that guides you in Blockchain Solutions project execution and control, then what should it NOT contain?

105. How well are you able to manage your risk?

106. What are the known stakeholder requirements?

107. What went right?

2.2 Scope Management Plan: Blockchain Solutions

108. Given the scope of the Blockchain Solutions project, which criterion should be optimized?

109. Organizational unit (e.g., department, team, or person) who will accept responsibility for satisfactory completion of the item?

110. Are estimating assumptions and constraints captured?

111. Are the appropriate IT resources adequate to meet planned commitments?

112. What problem is being solved by delivering this Blockchain Solutions project?

113. Process groups – where do scope management processes fit in?

114. Is the Blockchain Solutions project sponsor clearly communicating the business case or rationale for why this Blockchain Solutions project is needed?

115. Is the schedule updated on a periodic basis?

116. Are target dates established for each milestone deliverable?

117. Has your organization readiness assessment been conducted?

118. Cost / benefit analysis?

119. Is the steering committee active in Blockchain Solutions project oversight?

120. Have Blockchain Solutions project management standards and procedures been identified / established and documented?

121. Are the Blockchain Solutions project team members located locally to the users/stakeholders?

122. Has a capability assessment been conducted?

123. Does a documented Blockchain Solutions project organizational policy & plan (i.e. governance model) exist?

124. Can each item be appropriately scheduled?

125. Describe the process for rejecting the Blockchain Solutions project deliverables. What happens to rejected deliverables?

126. Is there an on-going process in place to monitor Blockchain Solutions project risks?

127. Are post milestone Blockchain Solutions project reviews (PMPR) conducted with your organization at least once a year?

2.3 Requirements Management Plan: Blockchain Solutions

128. Do you have an agreed upon process for alerting the Blockchain Solutions project Manager if a request for change in requirements leads to a product scope change?

129. Define the help desk model. who will take full responsibility?

130. Have stakeholders been instructed in the Change Control process?

131. Did you provide clear and concise specifications?

132. Which hardware or software, related to, or as outcome of the Blockchain Solutions project is new to your organization?

133. Is there formal agreement on who has authority to approve a change in requirements?

134. Subject to change control?

135. Is the system software (non-operating system) new to the IT Blockchain Solutions project team?

136. Will the product release be stable and mature enough to be deployed in the user community?

137. What is the earliest finish date for this Blockchain Solutions project if it is scheduled to start on ...?

138. How will requirements be managed?

139. Should you include sub-activities?

140. Will you document changes to requirements?

141. How do you know that you have done this right?

142. What went wrong?

143. Who will perform the analysis?

144. Who is responsible for monitoring and tracking the Blockchain Solutions project requirements?

145. How often will the reporting occur?

146. What performance metrics will be used?

2.4 Requirements Documentation: Blockchain Solutions

147. Validity. does the system provide the functions which best support the customers needs?

148. What variations exist for a process?

149. What is the risk associated with the technology?

150. How linear / iterative is your Requirements Gathering process (or will it be)?

151. Does the system provide the functions which best support the customers needs?

152. Is your business case still valid?

153. How will the proposed Blockchain Solutions project help?

154. Can the requirement be changed without a large impact on other requirements?

155. What are the potential disadvantages/ advantages?

156. If applicable; are there issues linked with the fact that this is an offshore Blockchain Solutions project?

157. What facilities must be supported by the system?

158. Where are business rules being captured?

159. What will be the integration problems?

160. How does what is being described meet the business need?

161. How do you get the user to tell you what they want?

162. Can you check system requirements?

163. What if the system wasn t implemented?

164. Has requirements gathering uncovered information that would necessitate changes?

165. What are the attributes of a customer?

166. Do technical resources exist?

2.5 Requirements Traceability Matrix: Blockchain Solutions

167. What is the WBS?

168. How do you manage scope?

169. How small is small enough?

170. Why do you manage scope?

171. Will you use a Requirements Traceability Matrix?

172. Describe the process for approving requirements so they can be added to the traceability matrix and Blockchain Solutions project work can be performed. Will the Blockchain Solutions project requirements become approved in writing?

173. Why use a WBS?

174. Is there a requirements traceability process in place?

175. How will it affect the stakeholders personally in career?

176. What percentage of Blockchain Solutions projects are producing traceability matrices between requirements and other work products?

177. Do you have a clear understanding of all subcontracts in place?

178. What are the chronologies, contingencies, consequences, criteria?

2.6 Project Scope Statement: Blockchain Solutions

179. Is the Blockchain Solutions project organization documented and on file?

180. Will statistics related to QA be collected, trends analyzed, and problems raised as issues?

181. Is there an information system for the Blockchain Solutions project?

182. Did your Blockchain Solutions project ask for this?

183. How often will scope changes be reviewed?

184. Will the risk plan be updated on a regular and frequent basis?

185. Have the reports to be produced, distributed, and filed been defined?

186. Was planning completed before the Blockchain Solutions project was initiated?

187. Are there adequate Blockchain Solutions project control systems?

188. Has the Blockchain Solutions project scope statement been reviewed as part of the baseline process?

189. Why do you need to manage scope?

190. Write a brief purpose statement for this Blockchain Solutions project. Include a business justification statement. What is the product of this Blockchain Solutions project?

191. Is the plan for your organization of the Blockchain Solutions project resources adequate?

192. What is a process you might recommend to verify the accuracy of the research deliverable?

193. Will the risk documents be filed?

194. Will all tasks resulting from issues be entered into the Blockchain Solutions project Plan and tracked through the plan?

195. Are there completion/verification criteria defined for each task producing an output?

196. How often do you estimate that the scope might change, and why?

197. Are there specific processes you will use to evaluate and approve/reject changes?

2.7 Assumption and Constraint Log: Blockchain Solutions

198. Are there procedures in place to effectively manage interdependencies with other Blockchain Solutions projects / systems?

199. Would known impacts serve as impediments?

200. Are processes for release management of new development from coding and unit testing, to integration testing, to training, and production defined and followed?

201. Have all stakeholders been identified?

202. Has a Blockchain Solutions project Communications Plan been developed?

203. Should factors be unpredictable over time?

204. Does the document/deliverable meet general requirements (for example, statement of work) for all deliverables?

205. Is this process still needed?

206. Does the document/deliverable meet all requirements (for example, statement of work) specific to this deliverable?

207. Are formal code reviews conducted?

208. Is there a Steering Committee in place?

209. Does a specific action and/or state that is known to violate security policy occur?

210. What do you audit?

211. Have all necessary approvals been obtained?

212. What weaknesses do you have?

213. Can the requirements be traced to the appropriate components of the solution, as well as test scripts?

214. Is the steering committee active in Blockchain Solutions project oversight?

215. What does an audit system look like?

216. No superfluous information or marketing narrative?

217. Are requirements management tracking tools and procedures in place?

2.8 Work Breakdown Structure: Blockchain Solutions

218. When would you develop a Work Breakdown Structure?

219. How big is a work-package?

220. What is the probability that the Blockchain Solutions project duration will exceed xx weeks?

221. Is the work breakdown structure (wbs) defined and is the scope of the Blockchain Solutions project clear with assigned deliverable owners?

222. Who has to do it?

223. When does it have to be done?

224. Where does it take place?

225. Why would you develop a Work Breakdown Structure?

226. Do you need another level?

227. How far down?

228. What is the probability of completing the Blockchain Solutions project in less that xx days?

229. When do you stop?

230. How will you and your Blockchain Solutions project team define the Blockchain Solutions projects scope and work breakdown structure?

231. What has to be done?

232. How much detail?

233. Why is it useful?

2.9 WBS Dictionary: Blockchain Solutions

234. Incurrence of actual indirect costs in excess of budgets, by element of expense?

235. Does the contractor use objective results, design reviews and tests to trace schedule performance?

236. What size should a work package be?

237. Knowledgeable Blockchain Solutions projections of future performance?

238. Are procedures in existence that control replanning of unopened work packages, and are corresponding procedures adhered to?

239. Is authorization of budgets in excess of the contract budget base controlled formally and done with the full knowledge and recognition of the procuring activity?

240. Are indirect costs charged to the appropriate indirect pools and incurring organization?

241. Are the requirements for all items of overhead established by rational, traceable processes?

242. Are current work performance indicators and goals relatable to original goals as modified by contractual changes, replanning, and reprogramming actions?

243. Are data elements reconcilable between internal summary reports and reports forwarded to us?

244. Detailed schedules which support control account and work package start and completion dates/events?

245. Does the scheduling system identify in a timely manner the status of work?

246. Are the procedures for identifying indirect costs to incurring organizations, indirect cost pools, and allocating the costs from the pools to the contracts formally documented?

247. Are the wbs and organizational levels for application of the Blockchain Solutions projected overhead costs identified?

248. Is each control account assigned to a single organizational element directly responsible for the work and identifiable to a single element of the CWBS?

249. What is wrong with this Blockchain Solutions project?

250. Can the contractor substantiate work package and planning package budgets?

251. Does the contractor require sufficient detailed planning of control accounts to constrain the application of budget initially allocated for future effort to current effort?

252. Are meaningful indicators identified for use in measuring the status of cost and schedule performance?

253. The already stated responsible for overhead performance control of related costs?

2.10 Schedule Management Plan: Blockchain Solutions

254. Are the schedule estimates reasonable given the Blockchain Solutions project?

255. Is the schedule vertically and horizontally traceable?

256. Are vendor invoices audited for accuracy before payment?

257. Are changes in deliverable commitments agreed to by all affected groups & individuals?

258. Are the processes for status updates and maintenance defined?

259. Has the ims content been baselined and is it adequately controlled?

260. Time for overtime?

261. Does the resource management plan include a personnel development plan?

262. Is your organization certified as a supplier, wholesaler and/or regular dealer?

263. Blockchain Solutions project definition & scope?

264. Personnel with expertise?

265. List all schedule constraints here. Must the Blockchain Solutions project be complete by a specified date?

266. Perform reality checks on schedules – are all tasks included?

267. What strengths do you have?

268. Can be realistically shortened (the duration of subsequent tasks)?

269. Are the activity durations realistic and at an appropriate level of detail for effective management?

270. Is the critical path valid?

271. Is the schedule feasible and at what cost?

272. What will be the format of the schedule model?

273. Is there a formal process for updating the Blockchain Solutions project baseline?

2.11 Activity List: Blockchain Solutions

274. What went well?

275. What is your organizations history in doing similar activities?

276. How much slack is available in the Blockchain Solutions project?

277. Who will perform the work?

278. When do the individual activities need to start and finish?

279. The wbs is developed as part of a joint planning session. and how do you know that youhave done this right?

280. How detailed should a Blockchain Solutions project get?

281. How do you determine the late start (LS) for each activity?

282. Where will it be performed?

283. How difficult will it be to do specific activities on this Blockchain Solutions project?

284. What did not go as well?

285. How should ongoing costs be monitored to try to keep the Blockchain Solutions project within budget?

286. What are the critical bottleneck activities?

287. Are the required resources available or need to be acquired?

288. In what sequence?

289. What is the total time required to complete the Blockchain Solutions project if no delays occur?

290. Can you determine the activity that must finish, before this activity can start?

291. Is infrastructure setup part of your Blockchain Solutions project?

2.12 Activity Attributes: Blockchain Solutions

292. Resources to accomplish the work?

293. Activity: fair or not fair?

294. Where else does it apply?

295. Is there anything planned that does not need to be here?

296. How else could the items be grouped?

297. What is missing?

298. Have you identified the Activity Leveling Priority code value on each activity?

299. Can more resources be added?

300. What is the general pattern here?

301. Has management defined a definite timeframe for the turnaround or Blockchain Solutions project window?

302. How many resources do you need to complete the work scope within a limit of X number of days?

303. Why?

304. What conclusions/generalizations can you draw

from this?

305. Is there a trend during the year?

306. What activity do you think you should spend the most time on?

307. Resource is assigned to?

2.13 Milestone List: Blockchain Solutions

308. Environmental effects?

309. Sustaining internal capabilities?

310. Which path is the critical path?

311. Insurmountable weaknesses?

312. How soon can the activity finish?

313. When will the Blockchain Solutions project be complete?

314. Describe your organizations strengths and core competencies. What factors will make your organization succeed?

315. What has been done so far?

316. What would happen if a delivery of material was one week late?

317. Describe the industry you are in and the market growth opportunities. What is the market for your technology, product or service?

318. Describe the concept of the technology, product or service that will be or has been developed. How will it be used?

319. Effects on core activities, distraction?

320. Do you foresee any technical risks or developmental challenges?

321. How difficult will it be to do specific activities on this Blockchain Solutions project?

322. Who will manage the Blockchain Solutions project on a day-to-day basis?

323. Marketing - reach, distribution, awareness?

324. How will the milestone be verified?

325. Level of the Innovation?

2.14 Network Diagram: Blockchain Solutions

326. If x is long, what would be the completion time if you break x into two parallel parts of y weeks and z weeks?

327. Will crashing x weeks return more in benefits than it costs?

328. What controls the start and finish of a job?

329. What activities must occur simultaneously with this activity?

330. What is the lowest cost to complete this Blockchain Solutions project in xx weeks?

331. How difficult will it be to do specific activities on this Blockchain Solutions project?

332. Planning: who, how long, what to do?

333. What are the Key Success Factors?

334. What is the probability of completing the Blockchain Solutions project in less that xx days?

335. What are the tools?

336. Review the logical flow of the network diagram. Take a look at which activities you have first and then sequence the activities. Do they make sense?

337. If the Blockchain Solutions project network diagram cannot change and you have extra personnel resources, what is the BEST thing to do?

338. What activities must follow this activity?

339. Are you on time?

340. Where do schedules come from?

341. How confident can you be in your milestone dates and the delivery date?

342. Where do you schedule uncertainty time?

343. What to do and When?

344. What are the Major Administrative Issues?

2.15 Activity Resource Requirements: Blockchain Solutions

345. What are constraints that you might find during the Human Resource Planning process?

346. Why do you do that?

347. When does monitoring begin?

348. Organizational Applicability?

349. How many signatures do you require on a check and does this match what is in your policy and procedures?

350. Other support in specific areas?

351. How do you manage time?

352. Which logical relationship does the PDM use most often?

353. Are there unresolved issues that need to be addressed?

354. Anything else?

355. Do you use tools like decomposition and rolling-wave planning to produce the activity list and other outputs?

356. What is the Work Plan Standard?

357. How do you handle petty cash?

2.16 Resource Breakdown Structure: Blockchain Solutions

358. Who delivers the information?

359. How can this help you with team building?

360. How difficult will it be to do specific activities on this Blockchain Solutions project?

361. Why do you do it?

362. What is each stakeholders desired outcome for the Blockchain Solutions project?

363. What defines a successful Blockchain Solutions project?

364. Changes based on input from stakeholders?

365. Why is this important?

366. What is the difference between % Complete and % work?

367. Who is allowed to perform which functions?

368. Who will use the system?

369. What is the number one predictor of a groups productivity?

370. Are the required resources available?

371. Goals for the Blockchain Solutions project. What is each stakeholders desired outcome for the Blockchain Solutions project?

372. Which resources should be in the resource pool?

373. What is Blockchain Solutions project communication management?

2.17 Activity Duration Estimates: Blockchain Solutions

374. Is the cost performance monitored to identify variances from the plan?

375. Will additional funds be needed for hardware or software?

376. Which is the BEST thing to do to try to complete a Blockchain Solutions project two days earlier?

377. What are the ways to create and distribute Blockchain Solutions project performance information?

378. Are Blockchain Solutions project records organized, maintained, and assessable by Blockchain Solutions project team members?

379. Are procedures defined for calculating cost estimates?

380. How does Blockchain Solutions project integration management relate to the Blockchain Solutions project life cycle, stakeholders, and the other Blockchain Solutions project management knowledge areas?

381. What is earned value?

382. Are adjustments implemented to correct or prevent defects?

383. Does a process exist to determine which risk events to accept and which events to disregard?

384. What are key inputs and outputs of the software?

385. What are the main processes included in Blockchain Solutions project quality management?

386. Are performance reviews conducted regularly to assess the status of Blockchain Solutions projects?

387. Do they make sense?

388. Why is it difficult to use Blockchain Solutions project management software well?

389. List five reasons why organizations outsource. Why is there a growing trend in outsourcing, especially in the government?

390. What is the shortest possible time it will take to complete this Blockchain Solutions project?

391. What are crucial elements of successful Blockchain Solutions project plan execution?

392. Which best describes how this affects the Blockchain Solutions project?

393. Who will promote it?

2.18 Duration Estimating Worksheet: Blockchain Solutions

394. What work will be included in the Blockchain Solutions project?

395. Is this operation cost effective?

396. How should ongoing costs be monitored to try to keep the Blockchain Solutions project within budget?

397. What info is needed?

398. Why estimate costs?

399. What is an Average Blockchain Solutions project?

400. When, then?

401. For other activities, how much delay can be tolerated?

402. What questions do you have?

403. What utility impacts are there?

404. Do any colleagues have experience with your organization and/or RFPs?

405. What is cost and Blockchain Solutions project cost management?

406. When does your organization expect to be able

to complete it?

407. Is a construction detail attached (to aid in explanation)?

408. Why estimate time and cost?

409. Will the Blockchain Solutions project collaborate with the local community and leverage resources?

410. Value pocket identification & quantification what are value pockets?

2.19 Project Schedule: Blockchain Solutions

411. Why is software Blockchain Solutions project disaster so common?

412. If there are any qualifying green components to this Blockchain Solutions project, what portion of the total Blockchain Solutions project cost is green?

413. Are quality inspections and review activities listed in the Blockchain Solutions project schedule(s)?

414. Is Blockchain Solutions project work proceeding in accordance with the original Blockchain Solutions project schedule?

415. How do you know that youhave done this right?

416. How many levels?

417. Why do you need to manage Blockchain Solutions project Risk?

418. Why time management?

419. How effectively were issues able to be resolved without impacting the Blockchain Solutions project Schedule or Budget?

420. Master Blockchain Solutions project schedule?

421. Are activities connected because logic dictates

the order in which others occur?

422. How can you shorten the schedule?

423. Why do you think schedule issues often cause the most conflicts on Blockchain Solutions projects?

424. What does that mean?

425. Is there a Schedule Management Plan that establishes the criteria and activities for developing, monitoring and controlling the Blockchain Solutions project schedule?

426. Why do you need schedules?

427. It allows the Blockchain Solutions project to be delivered on schedule. How Do you Use Schedules?

428. Month Blockchain Solutions project take?

2.20 Cost Management Plan: Blockchain Solutions

429. Has the scope management document been updated and distributed to help prevent scope creep?

430. Are tasks tracked by hours?

431. Were Blockchain Solutions project team members involved in detailed estimating and scheduling?

432. Responsibilities – what is the split of responsibilities between the owner and contractors?

433. Has a sponsor been identified?

434. Are Blockchain Solutions project team members committed fulltime?

435. Is your organization certified as a supplier, wholesaler, regular dealer, or manufacturer of corresponding products/supplies?

436. What are the nine areas of expertise?

437. Planning and scheduling responsibilities – How will the responsibilities for planning and scheduling be allocated?

438. Have adequate resources been provided by management to ensure Blockchain Solutions project success?

439. What would you do differently what did not work?

440. What does this mean to a cost or scheduler manager?

441. Has a resource management plan been created?

442. Are decisions captured in a decisions log?

443. Eac -estimate at completion, what is the total job expected to cost?

444. Exclusions – is there scope to be performed or provided by others?

445. Are action items captured and managed?

446. Escalation criteria met?

2.21 Activity Cost Estimates: Blockchain Solutions

447. How Award?

448. What procedures are put in place regarding bidding and cost comparisons, if any?

449. Who determines the quality and expertise of contractors?

450. What is procurement?

451. What are you looking for?

452. Did the consultant work with local staff to develop local capacity?

453. Was it performed on time?

454. What is the activity inventory?

455. When do you enter into PPM?

456. If you are asked to lower your estimate because the price is too high, what are your options?

457. Specific - is the objective clear in terms of what, how, when, and where the situation will be changed?

458. How many activities should you have?

459. Vac -variance at completion, how much over/

under budget do you expect to be?

460. Certification of actual expenditures?

461. How do you change activities?

462. What is the last item a Blockchain Solutions project manager must do to finalize Blockchain Solutions project close-out?

463. Are cost subtotals needed?

2.22 Cost Estimating Worksheet: Blockchain Solutions

464. What happens to any remaining funds not used?

465. How will the results be shared and to whom?

466. Who is best positioned to know and assist in identifying corresponding factors?

467. Is it feasible to establish a control group arrangement?

468. Identify the timeframe necessary to monitor progress and collect data to determine how the selected measure has changed?

469. What can be included?

470. What is the purpose of estimating?

471. Can a trend be established from historical performance data on the selected measure and are the criteria for using trend analysis or forecasting methods met?

472. What will others want?

473. What is the estimated labor cost today based upon this information?

474. Will the Blockchain Solutions project collaborate with the local community and leverage resources?

475. Is the Blockchain Solutions project responsive to community need?

476. What costs are to be estimated?

477. What additional Blockchain Solutions project(s) could be initiated as a result of this Blockchain Solutions project?

478. Ask: are others positioned to know, are others credible, and will others cooperate?

479. Does the Blockchain Solutions project provide innovative ways for stakeholders to overcome obstacles or deliver better outcomes?

2.23 Cost Baseline: Blockchain Solutions

480. How long are you willing to wait before you find out were late?

481. How likely is it to go wrong?

482. How will cost estimates be used?

483. What is the reality?

484. How difficult will it be to do specific tasks on the Blockchain Solutions project?

485. Does the suggested change request represent a desired enhancement to the products functionality?

486. Verify business objectives. Are others appropriate, and well-articulated?

487. If you sold 10x widgets on a day, what would the affect on profits be?

488. Have the resources used by the Blockchain Solutions project been reassigned to other units or Blockchain Solutions projects?

489. Have all the product or service deliverables been accepted by the customer?

490. At which frequency ?

491. Does the suggested change request seem to represent a necessary enhancement to the product?

492. Pcs for your new business. what would the life cycle costs be?

493. For what purpose ?

494. Who will use corresponding metrics ?

495. What can go wrong?

496. On time?

2.24 Quality Management Plan: Blockchain Solutions

497. Are you meeting the quality standards?

498. Sampling part of task?

499. What are your organizations current levels and trends for the already stated measures related to employee wellbeing, satisfaction, and development?

500. What are the appropriate test methods to be used?

501. Have all involved stakeholders and work groups committed to the Blockchain Solutions project?

502. What are your key performance measures/ indicators for tracking progress relative to your action plans?

503. Is there a Quality Management Plan?

504. Are you following the quality standards?

505. Results Available?

506. How do you ensure that protocols are up to date?

507. You know what your customers expectations are regarding this process?

508. What would you gain if you spent time working

to improve this process?

509. Contradictory information between different documents?

510. What does it do for you (or to me)?

511. Who is responsible for approving the qapp?

512. Meet how often?

513. Have Blockchain Solutions project management standards and procedures been established and documented?

514. Are qmps good forever?

515. What data do you gather/use/compile?

516. How is equipment calibrated?

2.25 Quality Metrics: Blockchain Solutions

517. What percentage are outcome-based?

518. Have risk areas been identified?

519. Is quality culture a competitive advantage?

520. Were quality attributes reported?

521. Are quality metrics defined?

522. Can visual measures help you to filter visualizations of interest?

523. What can manufacturing professionals do to ensure quality is seen as an integral part of the entire product lifecycle?

524. When is the security analysis testing complete?

525. The metrics–what is being considered?

526. What are your organizations next steps?

527. There are many reasons to shore up quality-related metrics, and what metrics are important?

528. Which are the right metrics to use?

529. How do you measure?

530. What method of measurement do you use?

531. Can you correlate your quality metrics to profitability?

532. Did evaluation start on time?

533. How exactly do you define when differences exist?

534. Is material complete (and does it meet the standards)?

535. Filter visualizations of interest?

536. How are requirements conflicts resolved?

2.26 Process Improvement Plan: Blockchain Solutions

537. What lessons have you learned so far?

538. Why do you want to achieve the goal?

539. Have the frequency of collection and the points in the process where measurements will be made been determined?

540. Why quality management?

541. Are you making progress on the goals?

542. Are you making progress on the improvement framework?

543. Where do you want to be?

544. Have the supporting tools been developed or acquired?

545. If a process improvement framework is being used, which elements will help the problems and goals listed?

546. Modeling current processes is great, and will you ever see a return on that investment?

547. Has the time line required to move measurement results from the points of collection to databases or users been established?

548. Does explicit definition of the measures exist?

549. What is the return on investment?

550. What personnel are the coaches for your initiative?

551. What makes people good SPI coaches?

552. Where are you now?

553. To elicit goal statements, do you ask a question such as, What do you want to achieve?

554. Are there forms and procedures to collect and record the data?

555. Does your process ensure quality?

2.27 Responsibility Assignment Matrix: Blockchain Solutions

556. Is work properly classified as measured effort, LOE, or apportioned effort and appropriately separated?

557. Availability – will the group or the person be available within the necessary time interval?

558. Identify and isolate causes of favorable and unfavorable cost and schedule variances?

559. Is every signing-off responsibility and every communicating responsibility critically necessary?

560. Who is responsible for work and budgets for each wbs?

561. Are the actual costs used for variance analysis reconcilable with data from the accounting system?

562. Changes in the direct base to which overhead costs are allocated?

563. Changes in the nature of the overhead requirements?

564. Where does all this information come from?

565. Direct labor dollars and/or hours?

566. Are overhead costs budgets established on a

basis consistent with anticipated direct business base?

567. The total budget for the contract (including estimates for authorized and unpriced work)?

568. Are control accounts opened and closed based on the start and completion of work contained therein?

569. All cwbs elements specified for external reporting?

570. Time-phased control account budgets?

571. What do you do when people do not respond?

572. Will too many Signing-off responsibilities delay the completion of the activity/deliverable?

573. Are all authorized tasks assigned to identified organizational elements?

2.28 Roles and Responsibilities: Blockchain Solutions

574. What expectations were NOT met?

575. Once the responsibilities are defined for the Blockchain Solutions project, have the deliverables, roles and responsibilities been clearly communicated to every participant?

576. Who is responsible for each task?

577. Who: who is involved?

578. Be specific; avoid generalities. Thank you and great work alone are insufficient. What exactly do you appreciate and why?

579. Have you ever been a part of this team?

580. Are the quality assurance functions and related roles and responsibilities clearly defined?

581. Who is involved?

582. Required skills, knowledge, experience?

583. Are governance roles and responsibilities documented?

584. Key conclusions and recommendations: Are conclusions and recommendations relevant and acceptable?

585. Implementation of actions: Who are the responsible units?

586. Attainable / achievable: the goal is attainable; can you actually accomplish the goal?

587. What expectations were met?

588. What should you highlight for improvement?

589. What is working well within your organizations performance management system?

590. What should you do now to ensure that you are exceeding expectations and excelling in your current position?

591. Are Blockchain Solutions project team roles and responsibilities identified and documented?

592. Was the expectation clearly communicated?

2.29 Human Resource Management Plan: Blockchain Solutions

593. Is Blockchain Solutions project work proceeding in accordance with the original Blockchain Solutions project schedule?

594. Is there an approved case?

595. Do all stakeholders know how to access this repository and where to find the Blockchain Solutions project documentation?

596. Is there an issues management plan in place?

597. How to convince employees that this is a necessary process?

598. Have adequate resources been provided by management to ensure Blockchain Solutions project success?

599. Have lessons learned been conducted after each Blockchain Solutions project release?

600. Were sponsors and decision makers available when needed outside regularly scheduled meetings?

601. What were things that you did very well and want to do the same again on the next Blockchain Solutions project?

602. Have reserves been created to address risks?

603. Are staff skills known and available for each task?

604. Responsiveness to change and the resulting demands for different skills and abilities?

605. Have all documents been archived in a Blockchain Solutions project repository for each release?

606. Is there a formal set of procedures supporting Stakeholder Management?

607. Is quality monitored from the perspective of the customers needs and expectations?

608. Blockchain Solutions project definition & scope?

609. Measurable - are the targets measurable?

2.30 Communications Management Plan: Blockchain Solutions

610. Do you prepare stakeholder engagement plans?

611. Do you ask; can you recommend others for you to talk with about this initiative?

612. What communications method?

613. What to know?

614. Why do you manage communications?

615. Is there an important stakeholder who is actively opposed and will not receive messages?

616. What to learn?

617. Who are the members of the governing body?

618. Will messages be directly related to the release strategy or phases of the Blockchain Solutions project?

619. Who have you worked with in past, similar initiatives?

620. Is the stakeholder role recognized by your organization?

621. Who to share with?

622. How did the term stakeholder originate?

623. Which team member will work with each stakeholder?

624. Who to learn from?

625. Where do team members get information?

626. What is Blockchain Solutions project communications management?

627. How were corresponding initiatives successful?

628. Which stakeholders are thought leaders, influences, or early adopters?

629. In your work, how much time is spent on stakeholder identification?

2.31 Risk Management Plan: Blockchain Solutions

630. Market risk -will the new service or product be useful to your organization or marketable to others?

631. Are staff committed for the duration of the product?

632. Risk categories: what are the main categories of risks that should be addressed on this Blockchain Solutions project?

633. Are tool mentors available?

634. Financial risk: can your organization afford to undertake the Blockchain Solutions project?

635. Methodology: how will risk management be performed on this Blockchain Solutions project?

636. Does the customer understand the software process?

637. How is risk response planning performed?

638. What things might go wrong?

639. Are tools for analysis and design available?

640. Are testing tools available and suitable?

641. Can the risk be avoided by choosing a different

alternative?

642. What are the chances the risk event will occur?

643. How much risk protection can you afford?

644. What should be done with non-critical risks?

645. Number of users of the product?

646. Have you worked with the customer in the past?

647. Can it be changed quickly?

648. Have top software and customer managers formally committed to support the Blockchain Solutions project?

649. How is risk identification performed?

2.32 Risk Register: Blockchain Solutions

650. How are risks graded?

651. How is a Community Risk Register created?

652. Contingency actions - planned actions to reduce the immediate seriousness of the risk when it does occur. What should you do when?

653. Risk documentation: what reporting formats and processes will be used for risk management activities?

654. Are there other alternative controls that could be implemented?

655. Which key risks have ineffective responses or outstanding improvement actions?

656. Can the likelihood and impact of failing to achieve corresponding recommendations and action plans be assessed?

657. What will be done?

658. Are your objectives at risk?

659. What could prevent you delivering on the strategic program objectives and what is being done to mitigate corresponding issues?

660. Are corrective measures implemented as

planned?

661. Do you require further engagement?

662. What is your current and future risk profile?

663. What should the audit role be in establishing a risk management process?

664. What risks might negatively or positively affect achieving the Blockchain Solutions project objectives?

665. What is the probability and impact of the risk occurring?

666. Are there any gaps in the evidence?

667. What is the reason for current performance gaps and do the risks and opportunities identified previously account for this?

668. Budget and schedule: what are the estimated costs and schedules for performing risk-related activities?

2.33 Probability and Impact Assessment: Blockchain Solutions

669. Do you use any methods to analyze risks?

670. What can you do to minimize the impact if it does?

671. Is the customer technically sophisticated in the product area?

672. Risk categorization -which of your categories has more risk than others?

673. Are Blockchain Solutions project requirements stable?

674. Do the people have the right combinations of skills?

675. What risks are necessary to achieve success?

676. How do the products attain the specifications?

677. What are the probabilities of chosen technologies being suitable for local conditions?

678. Mitigation -how can you avoid the risk?

679. Are the software tools integrated with each other?

680. How much risk do others need to take?

681. What should be the requirement of organizational restructuring as each subBlockchain Solutions project goes through a different lifecycle phase?

682. How would you suggest monitoring for risk transition indicators?

683. Do benefits and chances of success outweigh potential damage if success is not attained?

684. How risk averse are you?

685. Costs associated with late delivery or a defective product?

686. Assumptions analysis -what assumptions have you made or been given about your Blockchain Solutions project?

687. Who will be responsible for a slippage?

688. Are flexibility and reuse paramount?

2.34 Probability and Impact Matrix: Blockchain Solutions

689. My Blockchain Solutions project leader has suddenly left your organization, what do you do?

690. What is the impact if the risk does occur?

691. How well is the risk understood?

692. Do you have a consistent repeatable process that is actually used?

693. What are the methods to deal with risks?

694. Do others match with the clients requirement?

695. What needs to be DONE?

696. What is the risk appetite?

697. How is the Blockchain Solutions project going to be managed?

698. Are staff committed for the duration of the Blockchain Solutions project?

699. How carefully have the potential competitors been identified?

700. Are you on schedule?

701. What are the chances the risk events will occur?

702. Brain storm – mind maps, what if?

703. Which is the BEST thing to do?

704. Are the best people available?

705. What are the chances the event will occur?

706. Who are the owners?

2.35 Risk Data Sheet: Blockchain Solutions

707. How can hazards be reduced?

708. What are you weak at and therefore need to do better?

709. If it happens, what are the consequences?

710. Has the most cost-effective solution been chosen?

711. How reliable is the data source?

712. What if client refuses?

713. Are new hazards created?

714. What was measured?

715. Whom do you serve (customers)?

716. What are the main opportunities available to you that you should grab while you can?

717. Do effective diagnostic tests exist?

718. During work activities could hazards exist?

719. What are you here for (Mission)?

720. What will be the consequences if the risk

happens?

721. Will revised controls lead to tolerable risk levels?

722. What is the environment within which you operate (social trends, economic, community values, broad based participation, national directions etc.)?

723. What is the chance that it will happen?

724. What is the likelihood of it happening?

725. What will be the consequences if it happens?

2.36 Procurement Management Plan: Blockchain Solutions

726. What are things that you need to improve?

727. Are the key elements of a Blockchain Solutions project Charter present?

728. Is there an on-going process in place to monitor Blockchain Solutions project risks?

729. Are parking lot items captured?

730. In which phase of the Acquisition Process Cycle does source qualifications reside?

731. Has the Blockchain Solutions project scope been baselined?

732. Has a Blockchain Solutions project Communications Plan been developed?

733. How will multiple providers be managed?

734. Is there a requirements change management processes in place?

735. Were Blockchain Solutions project team members involved in the development of activity & task decomposition?

736. Was the scope definition used in task sequencing?

737. Does the Blockchain Solutions project have a formal Blockchain Solutions project Charter?

738. Are non-critical path items updated and agreed upon with the teams?

739. Are decisions made in a timely manner?

740. What is a Blockchain Solutions project Management Plan?

741. Do all stakeholders know how to access the PM repository and where to find the Blockchain Solutions project documentation?

742. Are trade-offs between accepting the risk and mitigating the risk identified?

743. Has the Blockchain Solutions project manager been identified?

2.37 Source Selection Criteria: Blockchain Solutions

744. Does your documentation identify why the team concurs or differs with reported performance from past performance report (CPARs, questionnaire responses, etc.)?

745. Are types/quantities of material, facilities appropriate?

746. How do you ensure an integrated assessment of proposals?

747. What documentation is necessary regarding electronic communications?

748. How do you encourage efficiency and consistency?

749. Do you want to wait until all offerors have been evaluated?

750. How is past performance evaluated?

751. Are resultant proposal revisions allowed?

752. What can not be disclosed?

753. What should be the contracting officers strategy?

754. What is the last item a Blockchain Solutions project manager must do to finalize Blockchain

Solutions project close-out?

755. What risks were identified in the proposals?

756. What does a sample rating scale look like?

757. How do you consolidate reviews and analysis of evaluators?

758. What documentation is needed for a tradeoff decision?

759. Can you prevent comparison of proposals?

760. Do you have a plan to document consensus results including disposition of any disagreement by individual evaluators?

761. Can you identify proposed teaming partners and/ or subcontractors and consider the nature and extent of proposed involvement in satisfying the Blockchain Solutions project requirements?

762. When and what information can be considered with offerors regarding past performance?

763. Who must be notified?

2.38 Stakeholder Management Plan: Blockchain Solutions

764. How accurate and complete is the information?

765. Are all vendor contracts closed out?

766. Is the current scope of the Blockchain Solutions project substantially different than that originally defined?

767. Where will verification occur, and by whom?

768. Are there standards for code development?

769. Are all resource assumptions documented?

770. Detail warranty and/or maintenance periods?

771. Why would you develop a Blockchain Solutions project Business Plan?

772. Alignment to strategic goals & objectives?

773. What is to be the method of release?

774. Does the system design reflect the requirements?

775. Are you meeting your customers expectations consistently?

776. Can you perform this task or activity in a more effective manner?

777. What information should be collected?

778. What are the advantages and disadvantages of using external contracted resources?

779. Has the business need been clearly defined?

780. Is there a formal set of procedures supporting Issues Management?

2.39 Change Management Plan: Blockchain Solutions

781. Has the training provider been established?

782. Have the systems been configured and tested?

783. What risks may occur upfront, during implementation and after implementation?

784. Will the culture embrace or reject this change?

785. Who is responsible for which tasks?

786. When developing your communication plan do you address : When should the given message be communicated?

787. Who might present the most resistance?

788. Is a training information sheet available?

789. What are the major changes to processes?

790. What are the specific target groups / audience that will be impacted by this change?

791. Who is the target audience of the piece of information?

792. What are the training strategies?

793. What new competencies will be required for the

roles?

794. What is the reason for the communication?

795. Has a training need analysis been carried out?

796. Have the business unit contacts been selected and notified?

797. What skills, education, knowledge, or work experiences should the resources have for each identified competency?

798. Which relationships will change?

799. Who in the business it includes?

800. What prerequisite knowledge or training is required?

3.0 Executing Process Group: Blockchain Solutions

801. Do the products created live up to the necessary quality?

802. Do Blockchain Solutions project managers understand your organizational context for Blockchain Solutions projects?

803. How many different communication channels does the Blockchain Solutions project team have?

804. What were things that you did well, and could improve, and how?

805. In what way has the program come up with innovative measures for problem-solving?

806. What are the Blockchain Solutions project management deliverables of each process group?

807. When do you share the scorecard with managers?

808. Who are the Blockchain Solutions project stakeholders?

809. How can software assist in procuring goods and services?

810. If a risk event occurs, what will you do?

811. How could you control progress of your Blockchain Solutions project?

812. What were things that you need to improve?

813. What are the key components of the Blockchain Solutions project communications plan?

814. How do you enter durations, link tasks, and view critical path information?

815. Based on your Blockchain Solutions project communication management plan, what worked well?

816. Do schedule issues conflicts?

817. What is the product of your Blockchain Solutions project?

818. Would you rate yourself as being risk-averse, risk-neutral, or risk-seeking?

819. What are the critical steps involved with strategy mapping?

3.1 Team Member Status Report: Blockchain Solutions

820. Will the staff do training or is that done by a third party?

821. Does your organization have the means (staff, money, contract, etc.) to produce or to acquire the product, good, or service?

822. Are the products of your organizations Blockchain Solutions projects meeting customers objectives?

823. Do you have an Enterprise Blockchain Solutions project Management Office (EPMO)?

824. How can you make it practical?

825. Are your organizations Blockchain Solutions projects more successful over time?

826. Are the attitudes of staff regarding Blockchain Solutions project work improving?

827. How does this product, good, or service meet the needs of the Blockchain Solutions project and your organization as a whole?

828. What specific interest groups do you have in place?

829. The problem with Reward & Recognition

Programs is that the truly deserving people all too often get left out. How can you make it practical?

830. Does the product, good, or service already exist within your organization?

831. How much risk is involved?

832. Why is it to be done?

833. When a teams productivity and success depend on collaboration and the efficient flow of information, what generally fails them?

834. Does every department have to have a Blockchain Solutions project Manager on staff?

835. How it is to be done?

836. Is there evidence that staff is taking a more professional approach toward management of your organizations Blockchain Solutions projects?

837. How will resource planning be done?

838. What is to be done?

3.2 Change Request: Blockchain Solutions

839. How fast will change requests be approved?

840. Screen shots or attachments included in a Change Request?

841. Who has responsibility for approving and ranking changes?

842. How are the measures for carrying out the change established?

843. Will this change conflict with other requirements changes (e.g., lead to conflicting operational scenarios)?

844. Who is responsible to authorize changes?

845. How does a team identify the discrete elements of a configuration?

846. Can you answer what happened, who did it, when did it happen, and what else will be affected?

847. Are you implementing itil processes?

848. Have scm procedures for noting the change, recording it, and reporting it been followed?

849. What is the relationship between requirements attributes and attributes like complexity and size?

850. What has an inspector to inspect and to check?

851. Have all related configuration items been properly updated?

852. Who can suggest changes?

853. Has a formal technical review been conducted to assess technical correctness?

854. Are there requirements attributes that are strongly related to the complexity and size?

855. How do you get changes (code) out in a timely manner?

856. Who needs to approve change requests?

857. What are the requirements for urgent changes?

3.3 Change Log: Blockchain Solutions

858. Is the change request open, closed or pending?

859. Who initiated the change request?

860. How does this change affect scope?

861. Do the described changes impact on the integrity or security of the system?

862. How does this change affect the timeline of the schedule?

863. When was the request submitted?

864. When was the request approved?

865. Is this a mandatory replacement?

866. Should a more thorough impact analysis be conducted?

867. Is the requested change request a result of changes in other Blockchain Solutions project(s)?

868. Where do changes come from?

869. Is the submitted change a new change or a modification of a previously approved change?

870. Is the change request within Blockchain Solutions project scope?

871. Is the change backward compatible without limitations?

872. How does this relate to the standards developed for specific business processes?

873. Will the Blockchain Solutions project fail if the change request is not executed?

3.4 Decision Log: Blockchain Solutions

874. What is your overall strategy for quality control / quality assurance procedures?

875. Do strategies and tactics aimed at less than full control reduce the costs of management or simply shift the cost burden?

876. How effective is maintaining the log at facilitating organizational learning?

877. Does anything need to be adjusted?

878. How do you know when you are achieving it?

879. What is the average size of your matters in an applicable measurement?

880. Who will be given a copy of this document and where will it be kept?

881. What alternatives/risks were considered?

882. What are the cost implications?

883. Meeting purpose; why does this team meet?

884. How does provision of information, both in terms of content and presentation, influence acceptance of alternative strategies?

885. At what point in time does loss become unacceptable?

886. How do you define success?

887. It becomes critical to track and periodically revisit both operational effectiveness; Are you noticing all that you need to, and are you interpreting what you see effectively?

888. Is your opponent open to a non-traditional workflow, or will it likely challenge anything you do?

889. What makes you different or better than others companies selling the same thing?

890. Linked to original objective?

891. What is the line where eDiscovery ends and document review begins?

892. Which variables make a critical difference?

893. How does an increasing emphasis on cost containment influence the strategies and tactics used?

3.5 Quality Audit: Blockchain Solutions

894. Are people allowed to contribute ideas?

895. Have personnel cleanliness and health requirements been established?

896. What happens if your organization fails its Quality Audit?

897. How does your organization know that its management system is appropriately effective and constructive?

898. How does your organization know that its systems for communicating with and among staff are appropriately effective and constructive?

899. How does your organization know that its management of its ethical responsibilities is appropriately effective and constructive?

900. How does your organization know that its system for governing staff behaviour is appropriately effective and constructive?

901. How does your organization know that its processes for managing severance are appropriately effective, constructive and fair?

902. What has changed/improved as a result of the review processes?

903. What does an analysis of your organizations staff profile suggest in terms of its planning, and how is this being addressed?

904. Statements of intent remain exactly that until they are put into effect. The next step is to deploy the already stated intentions. In other words, do the plans happen in reality?

905. How does your organization know that its financial management system is appropriately effective and constructive?

906. How does your organization know that its system for managing intellectual property issues is appropriately effective, constructive and fair?

907. What is the collective experience of the team to be assigned to an audit?

908. Do the suppliers use a formal quality system?

909. Are all employees made aware of device defects which may occur from the improper performance of specific jobs?

910. Health and safety arrangements; stress management workshops. How does your organization know that it provides a safe and healthy environment?

911. How does your organization know that its relationship with its (past) staff is appropriately effective and constructive?

912. How do staff know if they are doing a good job?

913. How does your organization know that its promotions system is appropriately effective, constructive and fair?

3.6 Team Directory: Blockchain Solutions

914. Who will talk to the customer?

915. Process decisions: are contractors adequately prosecuting the work?

916. Have you decided when to celebrate the Blockchain Solutions projects completion date?

917. What are you going to deliver or accomplish?

918. Contract requirements complied with?

919. Why is the work necessary?

920. Days from the time the issue is identified?

921. Decisions: is the most suitable form of contract being used?

922. How do unidentified risks impact the outcome of the Blockchain Solutions project?

923. Where will the product be used and/or delivered or built when appropriate?

924. Does a Blockchain Solutions project team directory list all resources assigned to the Blockchain Solutions project?

925. Who will write the meeting minutes and

distribute?

926. Who are your stakeholders (customers, sponsors, end users, team members)?

927. Process decisions: how well was task order work performed?

928. When will you produce deliverables?

929. What needs to be communicated?

930. Process decisions: are all start-up, turn over and close out requirements of the contract satisfied?

931. Decisions: what could be done better to improve the quality of the constructed product?

932. Who are the Team Members?

3.7 Team Operating Agreement: Blockchain Solutions

933. Resource allocation: how will individual team members account for time and expenses, and how will this be allocated in the team budget?

934. Are team roles clearly defined and accepted?

935. Do you leverage technology engagement tools group chat, polls, screen sharing, etc.?

936. What is the number of cases currently teamed?

937. Reimbursements: how will the team members be reimbursed for expenses and time commitments?

938. Do you prevent individuals from dominating the meeting?

939. Why does your organization want to participate in teaming?

940. What is a Virtual Team?

941. Have you set the goals and objectives of the team?

942. Must your members collaborate successfully to complete Blockchain Solutions projects?

943. Is compensation based on team and individual performance?

944. Do team members need to frequently communicate as a full group to make timely decisions?

945. Does your team need access to all documents and information at all times?

946. What are the safety issues/risks that need to be addressed and/or that the team needs to consider?

947. Do you use a parking lot for any items that are important and outside of the agenda?

948. Are there more than two functional areas represented by your team?

949. What is the anticipated procedure (recruitment, solicitation of volunteers, or assignment) for selecting team members?

950. What is your unique contribution to your organization?

951. How does teaming fit in with overall organizational goals and meet organizational needs?

3.8 Team Performance Assessment: Blockchain Solutions

952. To what degree can team members meet frequently enough to accomplish the teams ends?

953. To what degree do team members feel that the purpose of the team is important, if not exciting?

954. Individual task proficiency and team process behavior: what is important for team functioning?

955. How do you recognize and praise members for contributions?

956. To what degree does the team possess adequate membership to achieve its ends?

957. Can familiarity breed backup?

958. To what degree is there a sense that only the team can succeed?

959. To what degree will new and supplemental skills be introduced as the need is recognized?

960. What are you doing specifically to develop the leaders around you?

961. To what degree can all members engage in open and interactive considerations?

962. What makes opportunities more or less obvious?

963. What is method variance?

964. Effects of crew composition on crew performance: Does the whole equal the sum of its parts?

965. How hard did you try to make a good selection?

966. When does the medium matter?

967. To what degree can the team measure progress against specific goals?

968. To what degree are the teams goals and objectives clear, simple, and measurable?

969. To what degree do team members agree with the goals, relative importance, and the ways in which achievement will be measured?

970. To what degree does the teams work approach provide opportunity for members to engage in fact-based problem solving?

3.9 Team Member Performance Assessment: Blockchain Solutions

971. What evidence supports your decision-making?

972. How do you know that all team members are learning?

973. How is the timing of assessments organized (e.g., pre/post-test, single point during training, multiple reassessment during training)?

974. What stakeholders must be involved in the development and oversight of the performance plan?

975. Are the draft goals SMART ?

976. What happens if a team member disagrees with the Job Expectations?

977. How do you create a self-sustaining capacity for a collaborative culture?

978. To what degree are the goals ambitious?

979. Does adaptive training work?

980. How effective is training that is delivered through technology-based platforms?

981. What, if any, steps are available for employees who feel they have been unfairly or inaccurately rated?

982. What is the target group for instruction (e.g., individual and collective or small team instruction)?

983. Who is responsible?

984. What is collaboration?

985. Are any validation activities performed?

986. Should a ratee get a copy of all the raters documents about the employees performance?

987. Did training work?

988. Does platform-specific assessment information contribute to training placement or tailoring of instruction (e.g. aptitude-treatment interaction)?

989. Why were corresponding selected?

3.10 Issue Log: Blockchain Solutions

990. Persistence; will users learn a work around or will they be bothered every time?

991. What are the stakeholders interrelationships?

992. Is the issue log kept in a safe place?

993. Who is the stakeholder?

994. Why multiple evaluators?

995. How do you reply to this question; you am new here and managing this major program. How do you suggest you build your network?

996. How often do you engage with stakeholders?

997. What is the stakeholders level of authority?

998. Who is the issue assigned to?

999. What approaches to you feel are the best ones to use?

1000. What is a Stakeholder?

1001. How do you manage human resources?

1002. Is access to the Issue Log controlled?

1003. Why not more evaluators?

1004. Who reported the issue?

4.0 Monitoring and Controlling Process Group: Blockchain Solutions

1005. Are there areas that need improvement?

1006. How well did the chosen processes produce the expected results?

1007. Is there sufficient time allotted between the general system design and the detailed system design phases?

1008. Does the solution fit in with organizations technical architectural requirements?

1009. What good practices or successful experiences or transferable examples have been identified?

1010. How is agile Blockchain Solutions project management done?

1011. Key stakeholders to work with. How many potential communications channels exist on the Blockchain Solutions project?

1012. Is progress on outcomes due to your program?

1013. Propriety: who needs to be involved in the evaluation to be ethical?

1014. What business situation is being addressed?

1015. What were things that you did very well and

want to do the same again on the next Blockchain Solutions project?

1016. Feasibility: how much money, time, and effort can you put into this?

1017. Is there adequate validation on required fields?

1018. How do you monitor progress?

1019. How well defined and documented were the Blockchain Solutions project management processes you chose to use?

1020. What kinds of things in particular are you looking for data on?

1021. Who needs to be involved in the planning?

1022. Do the partners have sufficient financial capacity to keep up the benefits produced by the programme?

1023. Where is the Risk in the Blockchain Solutions project?

4.1 Project Performance Report: Blockchain Solutions

1024. To what degree are the demands of the task compatible with and converge with the mission and functions of the formal organization?

1025. To what degree does the teams approach to its work allow for modification and improvement over time?

1026. To what degree do team members articulate the teams work approach?

1027. To what degree are the goals realistic?

1028. To what degree are the demands of the task compatible with and converge with the relationships of the informal organization?

1029. To what degree does the teams purpose constitute a broader, deeper aspiration than just accomplishing short-term goals?

1030. To what degree will the approach capitalize on and enhance the skills of all team members in a manner that takes into consideration other demands on members of the team?

1031. What is the PRS?

1032. What is the degree to which rules govern information exchange between groups?

1033. To what degree does the teams purpose contain themes that are particularly meaningful and memorable?

1034. To what degree does the informal organization make use of individual resources and meet individual needs?

1035. To what degree are the tasks requirements reflected in the flow and storage of information?

1036. To what degree can the team ensure that all members are individually and jointly accountable for the teams purpose, goals, approach, and work-products?

1037. To what degree will the team ensure that all members equitably share the work essential to the success of the team?

1038. To what degree can the cognitive capacity of individuals accommodate the flow of information?

1039. To what degree are fresh input and perspectives systematically caught and added (for example, through information and analysis, new members, and senior sponsors)?

1040. To what degree do team members understand one anothers roles and skills?

1041. To what degree does the teams work approach provide opportunity for members to engage in open interaction?

1042. To what degree is the team cognizant of small wins to be celebrated along the way?

4.2 Variance Analysis: Blockchain Solutions

1043. Do work packages consist of discrete tasks which are adequately described?

1044. Who is generally responsible for monitoring and taking action on variances?

1045. What can be the cause of an increase in costs?

1046. Does the contractors system provide unit or lot costs when applicable?

1047. What is the actual cost of work performed?

1048. There are detailed schedules which support control account and work package start and completion dates/events?

1049. Are all elements of indirect expense identified to overhead cost budgets of Blockchain Solutions projections?

1050. When, during the last four quarters, did a primary business event occur causing a fluctuation?

1051. Are all cwbs elements specified for external reporting?

1052. Budgeted cost for work performed?

1053. Are detailed work packages planned as far in

advance as practicable?

1054. Are overhead cost budgets established for each department which has authority to incur overhead costs?

1055. Wbs elements contractually specified for reporting of status to your organization (lowest level only)?

1056. What are the actual costs to date?

1057. Who are responsible for the establishment of budgets and assignment of resources for overhead performance?

1058. How do you identify and isolate causes of favorable and unfavorable cost and schedule variances?

1059. Are there changes in the direct base to which overhead costs are allocated?

1060. Are there changes in the overhead pool and/or organization structures?

1061. Are all budgets assigned to control accounts?

4.3 Earned Value Status: Blockchain Solutions

1062. How does this compare with other Blockchain Solutions projects?

1063. Earned value can be used in almost any Blockchain Solutions project situation and in almost any Blockchain Solutions project environment. it may be used on large Blockchain Solutions projects, medium sized Blockchain Solutions projects, tiny Blockchain Solutions projects (in cut-down form), complex and simple Blockchain Solutions projects and in any market sector. some people, of course, know all about earned value, they have used it for years - but perhaps not as effectively as they could have?

1064. How much is it going to cost by the finish?

1065. Are you hitting your Blockchain Solutions projects targets?

1066. Validation is a process of ensuring that the developed system will actually achieve the stakeholders desired outcomes; Are you building the right product? What do you validate?

1067. Verification is a process of ensuring that the developed system satisfies the stakeholders agreements and specifications; Are you building the product right? What do you verify?

1068. When is it going to finish?

1069. If earned value management (EVM) is so good in determining the true status of a Blockchain Solutions project and Blockchain Solutions project its completion, why is it that hardly any one uses it in information systems related Blockchain Solutions projects?

1070. Where is evidence-based earned value in your organization reported?

1071. Where are your problem areas?

1072. What is the unit of forecast value?

4.4 Risk Audit: Blockchain Solutions

1073. Have top software and customer managers formally committed to support the Blockchain Solutions project?

1074. Who is responsible for what?

1075. What expertise do auditors need to generate effective business-level risk assessments, and to what extent do auditors currently possess the already stated attributes?

1076. Are audit program plans risk-adjusted?

1077. What are the risks that could stop you from achieving your KPIs?

1078. Are all managers or operators of the facility or equipment competent or qualified?

1079. Is your organization able to present documentary evidence in support of compliance?

1080. Have reasonable steps been taken to reduce the risks to acceptable levels?

1081. When your organization is entering into a major contract, does it seek legal advice?

1082. Do you record and file all audits?

1083. How do you govern assets?

1084. Is a software Blockchain Solutions project management tool available?

1085. Are regular safety inspections made of buildings, grounds and equipment?

1086. Does your organization have or has considered the need for insurance covers: public liability, professional indemnity and directors and officers liability?

1087. Do you manage the process through use of metrics?

1088. Do you meet all obligations relating to funds secured from grants, loans and sponsors?

1089. What is happening in other jurisdictions? Could that happen here?

1090. Can analytical tests provide evidence that is as strong as evidence from traditional substantive tests?

1091. Are procedures developed to respond to foreseeable emergencies and communicated to all involved?

1092. Do you have an emergency plan?

4.5 Contractor Status Report: Blockchain Solutions

1093. What process manages the contracts?

1094. What are the minimum and optimal bandwidth requirements for the proposed solution?

1095. Are there contractual transfer concerns?

1096. How does the proposed individual meet each requirement?

1097. What is the average response time for answering a support call?

1098. How long have you been using the services?

1099. How is risk transferred?

1100. What was the overall budget or estimated cost?

1101. What was the actual budget or estimated cost for your organizations services?

1102. What was the budget or estimated cost for your organizations services?

1103. If applicable; describe your standard schedule for new software version releases. Are new software version releases included in the standard maintenance plan?

1104. What was the final actual cost?

1105. Who can list a Blockchain Solutions project as organization experience, your organization or a previous employee of your organization?

1106. Describe how often regular updates are made to the proposed solution. Are corresponding regular updates included in the standard maintenance plan?

4.6 Formal Acceptance: Blockchain Solutions

1107. How well did the team follow the methodology?

1108. Have all comments been addressed?

1109. Was business value realized?

1110. Does it do what client said it would?

1111. Was the client satisfied with the Blockchain Solutions project results?

1112. General estimate of the costs and times to complete the Blockchain Solutions project?

1113. How does your team plan to obtain formal acceptance on your Blockchain Solutions project?

1114. Who would use it?

1115. Do you perform formal acceptance or burn-in tests?

1116. Is formal acceptance of the Blockchain Solutions project product documented and distributed?

1117. Do you buy pre-configured systems or build your own configuration?

1118. Was the Blockchain Solutions project managed well?

1119. Does it do what Blockchain Solutions project team said it would?

1120. What are the requirements against which to test, Who will execute?

1121. What can you do better next time?

1122. What features, practices, and processes proved to be strengths or weaknesses?

1123. Was the sponsor/customer satisfied?

1124. What is the Acceptance Management Process?

1125. What function(s) does it fill or meet?

1126. Was the Blockchain Solutions project work done on time, within budget, and according to specification?

5.0 Closing Process Group: Blockchain Solutions

1127. Was the schedule met?

1128. Are there funding or time constraints?

1129. What areas were overlooked on this Blockchain Solutions project?

1130. What could have been improved?

1131. How critical is the Blockchain Solutions project success to the success of your organization?

1132. What areas does the group agree are the biggest success on the Blockchain Solutions project?

1133. Did the Blockchain Solutions project team have enough people to execute the Blockchain Solutions project plan?

1134. When will the Blockchain Solutions project be done?

1135. Can the lesson learned be replicated?

1136. What were the desired outcomes?

1137. How dependent is the Blockchain Solutions project on other Blockchain Solutions projects or work efforts?

1138. Did you do what you said you were going to do?

1139. Was the user/client satisfied with the end product?

1140. Were escalated issues resolved promptly?

1141. Did the Blockchain Solutions project management methodology work?

1142. Based on your Blockchain Solutions project communication management plan, what worked well?

1143. Is there a clear cause and effect between the activity and the lesson learned?

1144. Did the Blockchain Solutions project team have the right skills?

5.1 Procurement Audit: Blockchain Solutions

1145. When competitive dialogue was used, did the contracting authority provide sufficient justification for the use of this procedure and was the contract actually particularly complex?

1146. Where your organization engaged an expert, was the contract awarded in compliance with procurement regulations?

1147. Are receiving reports on file for all claims for equipment, supplies and materials in the paid claims file?

1148. Are decisions to outsource and being part of public private partnerships closely linked to the delivery of departments core services and functions?

1149. Is there no evidence of unauthorized release of information or seemingly unnecessary contacts with bidders personnel during the evaluation and negotiation processes?

1150. Are purchasing actions processed on a timely basis?

1151. Does the strategy ensure that appropriate controls are in place to ensure propriety and regularity in delivery?

1152. Is free and fair (international) competition

promoted by organizational policies and legislation, in line with legal, trade organizations and other policies?

1153. Is there a form specified for bids?

1154. Is a risk evaluation performed?

1155. Were any additional works or deliveries admissible without the need for a new procurement procedure?

1156. Does an appropriately qualified official check the quality of performance against the contract terms?

1157. Is the purchasing department consulted on favorable purchasing opportunities, economic ordering quantities, and revision of purchasing specifications?

1158. Do buyers obtain price quotations or bids from two or more suppliers on significant purchases if catalog or advertised prices are not available?

1159. Were all interested operators allowed the opportunity to participate?

1160. Do established procedures ensure that computer programs will not pay the same group of invoices twice?

1161. What is the process cost of the procurement function?

1162. Is a cash flow chart prepared and used in

determining the timing and term of investments?

1163. Does the department evaluate and benchmark the performance of the procurement function/ unit against other comparable procurement functions/ units?

1164. How do you address the risk of fraud and corruption?

5.2 Contract Close-Out: Blockchain Solutions

1165. Was the contract sufficiently clear so as not to result in numerous disputes and misunderstandings?

1166. Are the signers the authorized officials?

1167. Parties: Authorized?

1168. What is capture management?

1169. Change in knowledge?

1170. Have all contracts been completed?

1171. How/when used ?

1172. Parties: who is involved?

1173. Was the contract type appropriate?

1174. Change in attitude or behavior?

1175. Was the contract complete without requiring numerous changes and revisions?

1176. Have all acceptance criteria been met prior to final payment to contractors?

1177. Have all contract records been included in the Blockchain Solutions project archives?

1178. Has each contract been audited to verify acceptance and delivery?

1179. How does it work?

1180. Change in circumstances?

1181. What happens to the recipient of services?

1182. Have all contracts been closed?

1183. How is the contracting office notified of the automatic contract close-out?

5.3 Project or Phase Close-Out: Blockchain Solutions

1184. What could be done to improve the process?

1185. What was the preferred delivery mechanism?

1186. What is a Risk Management Process?

1187. What information did each stakeholder need to contribute to the Blockchain Solutions projects success?

1188. What process was planned for managing issues/risks?

1189. What hierarchical authority does the stakeholder have in your organization?

1190. Were messages directly related to the release strategy or phases of the Blockchain Solutions project?

1191. What was learned?

1192. When and how were information needs best met?

1193. What is the information level of detail required for each stakeholder?

1194. Who controlled key decisions that were made?

1195. Who is responsible for award close-out?

1196. Did the Blockchain Solutions project management methodology work?

1197. What are the mandatory communication needs for each stakeholder?

1198. If you were the Blockchain Solutions project sponsor, how would you determine which Blockchain Solutions project team(s) and/or individuals deserve recognition?

1199. Does the lesson educate others to improve performance?

1200. How often did each stakeholder need an update?

1201. What were the actual outcomes?

5.4 Lessons Learned: Blockchain Solutions

1202. How effective was the documentation that you received with the Blockchain Solutions project product/service?

1203. To what extent was the evolution of risks communicated?

1204. How long did redeployment take?

1205. How effective were the techniques used to prepare you and your organization for the impact of the changes brought about by the product or service produced by the Blockchain Solutions project?

1206. What is the value of the deliverable?

1207. What Blockchain Solutions project circumstances were not anticipated?

1208. What surprises did the team have to deal with?

1209. Overall, how effective were the efforts to prepare you and your organization for the impact of the product/service of the Blockchain Solutions project?

1210. Were the Blockchain Solutions project goals attained?

1211. What specialization does the task require?

1212. What is the frequency of group communications?

1213. How effectively were issues resolved before escalation was necessary?

1214. What is your organizations performance history?

1215. Are there any hidden conflicts of interest?

1216. Was the control overhead justified?

1217. How effective were your functional specs?

1218. Who managed most of the communication within the Blockchain Solutions project?

1219. What would you like to see better documented about how to use existing processes on this type of Blockchain Solutions project?

1220. How mature are the observations?

1221. Is the lesson significant, valid, and applicable?

Index

281

project 2-4, 6-8, 16, 18, 28, 46, 59, 61, 63, 84, 91, 95, 100, 105-107, 110-111, 115, 119, 122, 125-141, 143, 145-150, 152, 154-158, 160-163, 166-174, 177-180, 182-183, 190-197, 199-202, 206-210, 214-217, 220-221, 227, 237-239, 244-247, 249-253, 257, 259-262

projected 152

projects 2, 48, 112, 125, 128, 133, 143, 147, 150, 169, 173, 180, 214, 216-217, 227, 229, 244-245, 252, 259

promising 103

promote 53, 58, 131, 169

promoted 255

promotions 226

promptly 253

proofing 88

proper 95

properly 29, 34, 188, 219

property 225

proposal 208

proposals 97, 208-209

proposed 24, 47, 49, 78-79, 141, 209, 248-249

propriety 237, 254

protect 66, 121, 135

protected 68

protection 102, 197

protocols 182

proved 251

provide 21, 62, 115, 119, 123, 130, 139, 141, 179, 232, 240, 242, 247, 254

provided 11, 97, 131, 174-175, 192

provider 212

providers 75, 206

provides 225

providing 95, 130

provision 222

public 247, 254

publisher 1

pulled 112

purchase 7

purchases 255

purchasing 254-255

purpose 2, 9, 111, 146, 178, 181, 222, 231, 239-240

pushing 117

qualified 37, 60, 64, 70-71, 246, 255

qualifies 59, 70

301

CPSIA information can be obtained
at www.ICGtesting.com
Printed in the USA
BVHW041543230819
556561BV00043B/3351/P